Sabine Baring-Gould

English minstrelsie

a national monument of English song

Sabine Baring-Gould

English minstrelsie
a national monument of English song

ISBN/EAN: 9783741149962

Manufactured in Europe, USA, Canada, Australia, Japa

Cover: Foto ©Angelika Wolter / pixelio.de

Manufactured and distributed by brebook publishing software (www.brebook.com)

Sabine Baring-Gould

English minstrelsie

English Minstrelsie

A National Monument of English Song

COLLATED AND EDITED, WITH NOTES AND
HISTORICAL INTRODUCTIONS, BY

S. BARING-GOULD, M.A.

THE AIRS, IN BOTH NOTATIONS, ARRANGED BY
H. FLEETWOOD SHEPPARD, M.A.
F. W. BUSSELL, B.D., Mus. B. Oxon.; AND
W. H. HOPKINSON, A.R.C.O.

IN EIGHT VOLUMES
VOLUME THE FIRST

Edinburgh
T. C. & E. C. JACK, GRANGE PUBLISHING WORKS
1895

Dedicated
By Gracious Permission
to
Her Majesty the Queen

INDEX TO SONGS—Vol. I.

. In cases where the First Line differs from the Title, the former is also given (in italics). The figures in parentheses refer to the page at which the Note will be found.

A Master I have (xxx.)	76	LISTEN to the Voice of Love (xxix.) . .	44
Amo Amas (xxviii.) . . .	24	*Loud roar'd the Dreadful Thunder* (xxxii.)	111
A Schooling I went as a Boy (xxix.) .	42	Lubin's Rural Cot (xxx.) .	73
As Dolly sat Milking (xxvii.) . .	11		
At the Peaceful Midnight Hour (xxx.)	61	*Many have told of the Monks* (xxxii.) .	106
		Marigold Lane (xxix.) .	42
BAILIFF's Daughter, The (xxix.)	50	Monks of Old, The (xxxii.)	106
Bay of Biscay, The (xxxii.)	111	NORTHERN Lass, The (xxx., xxxi.)	66
CHARMING Phillis (xxvii.) .	8	*Old Simon the Cellarer* (xxxii.) . .	97
Cherry Ripe (xxix.) . .	36	O Listen, Listen to the Voice of Love (xxix.)	44
Come, if you dare (xxviii.) .	20		
Come, Lasses and Lads (xxviii.)	18	PASTIME with good Company (xxvii.)	4
Come, Take your Glass (xxx.) .	66	Poor Jack (xxxii.)	102
		Returning Home across the Fields (xxx.)	73
DAMSEL possessed of great Beauty, A (xxix.)	48	Rock'd in the Cradle of the Deep (xxxii.) .	92
Down among the Dead Men (xxix.) .	46		
		SHOULD he upbraid (xxx.) .	78
FARMER's Boy, The (xxx.) .	58	Simon the Cellarer (xxxii.) .	97
Flying Dutchman, The (xxxii.) .	88	Spider and the Fly, The (xxxii.) .	108
		Sweet Nelly, my Heart's Delight (xxx.)	56
GALLOPING Dreary Dun (xxx.) .	76		
Garden Gate, The (xxx.) .	84	TAKE a Bumper and try (xxix.) . .	30
Giles Scroggins (xxviii.) .	26	*The Day was closed, the Moon* (xxx.) .	84
God save the Queen (xxv.) . .	2	*There was a Youth* (xxix.) . .	50
Go patter to Lubbers and Swabs (xxxii.)	102	*The Sun had set behind the Hill* (xxx.)	58
		The Women all tell I'm false (xxix.) .	30
HENRY VIII.'s Song (xxvii.) .	4	'Twas on a very Stormy Day (xxxii.)	88
Here's a Health to the Queen (xxix.) .	46		
Here's to the Maiden (xxviii.)	28	VICAR of Bray, The (xxvii.)	14
		WE met, 'twas in a Crowd (xxxii.) . .	100
I AM a Friar of Orders Grey (xxix.) .	52	When once I was a Shepherd Boy (xxvii.)	6
I'm Afloat (xxxii.)	94	When that I was a little tiny Boy (xxxii.) .	86
In good King Charles's Golden Days (xxvii.)	14	Where the Bee Sucks (xxix.) . .	33
I've been roaming (xxx.) . .	68	"*Will you walk into my Parlour?*" (xxxii.)	108
I went to the Fair (xxix.) .	40	Wolf, The (xxx.) . .	61

MINSTRELS. *From Launceston Parish Church* (1521).

AN HISTORICAL SKETCH OF ENGLISH NATIONAL SONG

Self-depreciation among the English—In music dates from the reign of Charles I.—England at the close of the Middle Ages the most musical country in Europe—Part-singing began in England—Chaucer's testimony to the knowledge of music in England—Notices from the Romances of Chivalry—Songs adapted to several sorts of instruments—Three-part songs—Music in the Elizabethan Age—In that of the Restoration—Ballad-singing in the country—The Minstrels—The Crussol Company—Decline of the Minstrels—Itinerant Ballad-Singers—Minstrels put down by Act of Parliament—Character of melodies depends on the instrument to which accompanied—The Harp in England—The Bagpipe—Pipe and Tabour—The Hornpipe—The Lute—The Thrums—Fiddle and Crowd—Country Dances based on Ballad airs—Change that took place in the character of music—Scientific Music—The discovery of time in music—Fugue-writing—Contempt for melody among the scientific writers—They compose on popular themes and invent nothing—The Madrigal—The people retained their love of melody—The Restoration marked the end of the old formal scientific school and the restoration of melody—Influence of Lulli—Operatic music—Purcell—The Opera in England—Introduction of the Italian Opera into England—The revolt of English taste—The " Beggar's Opera "—Imitations—Arne—The Public Gardens—Engraved music—English music acquired much from contact with Italian music—Abandonment of the ancient modes—The authentic and plagal modes—The modern scale—The old modes still in use among the English peasantry—Handel's influence confined to oratorio—Arne possessed more in secular music—Haydn the founder of modern music—Mozart of the modern opera—English music had its tradition broken—Ballad operas of Arnold, Dibdin, Storace, Shield—Bishop—The singers Clifton, Hudson, Blewitt, and Horn—Moore's songs—Negro melodies—Song-books—D'Urfey—List of song-books—Preservation of early airs—In hymnody—The aim of the collection of " English Minstrelsie "—The charm of genuine English music.

T is one of the most characteristic features of the English people that they are ready to disparage whatever is of home growth, and to welcome what is foreign. I do not suppose that this feature is a very genuine one, but is acquired; it is an affectation that dates from the period when it was considered proper for a gentleman to make the grand tour. He returned from the Continent to turn up his nose at his old English manor-house, and to call in Italian architects to tear it down and substitute for it a Florentine pallazo. At the same time he professed to despise the music of Old England. Nothing would please his foppish ears save the compositions of the Italian musicians.

The preference accorded to foreign music began in the latter part of the reign of Charles I. It was commented on by Henry Lawes in 1653: "Wise men have observed our generation so giddy that whatsoever is native, be it never so excellent, must lose its taste, because they have lost theirs. . . . This present generation is so sated with what's native, that nothing takes their ear but what's sung in a language which, commonly, they understand as little as they do the music." And he goes on to relate how he took "an index of old Italian songs, and this, which read together made a strange medley of nonsense, he set to a varied air, and gave out that it came from Italy, whereby it passed for a rare Italian song."

Matthew Lock, also, to whom we owe the incomparable music to Macbeth, says, in 1656: " For those mountebanks of wit who think it necessary to disparage all they meet with of their own countrymen, I shall make bold to tell them, that I never yet saw any foreign instrumental composition (a few French corants excepted) worthy an Englishman's transcribing."

A

AN HISTORICAL SKETCH OF ENGLISH NATIONAL SONG

In Charles II.'s reign this disparagement of what was native grown, and exaltation of what was French or Italian, grew into a prevailing fashion; and the introduction of foreign singers, fiddlers, and dancers, tended largely to throw English artists as well as composers into the shade. When the leaders of fashion affected to despise English music, all the servile crew of imitators followed suit, and in 1782 Dr. Burney, who should have known better, and, indeed, did know better, was not ashamed to say of English music: "It is related that the Turks have a limited number of tunes, and the vocal music of our own country seems long to have been equally circumscribed; for till the last century, it seems as if the number of our secular and popular melodies did not greatly exceed that of the Turks," and, in a note, he adds that the tunes of the Turks were in all twenty-four.[1]

Actually England had, at the close of the Middle Ages, the character of being the very home and well-spring of music; and harmony in singing was customary in Britain long before it was so on the Continent. At the close of the seventeenth century, Giraldus Cambrensis, archdeacon, and afterwards Bishop of St. David's, gave the following testimony to the manner of singing of the Welsh and the inhabitants of the North of England: "The Britons do not sing their tunes in unison, like the inhabitants of other countries, but in different parts. So that, when a company of singers meets to sing, as is usual in this country, as many different parts are heard as there are singers. . . . In the Northern parts of Britain beyond the Humber, and on the borders of Yorkshire, the inhabitants make use of a similar kind of symphonious harmony in singing, but with only two differences or varieties of tune and voice; the one murmuring the under part, the other singing the upper in a manner equally soft and pleasing."

From this description of Giraldus, it is not difficult to understand that the Welsh employed a vocal harmony in many parts, led thereto by the harp, whereas in Northumbria the ballads were accompanied by a bass or drone, imitated from the bagpipe.

In 1159, when Thomas à Becket conducted the negotiations for the marriage of that arch-scoundrel, Henry Courtmantel, with the daughter of Louis VII., and went to Paris as Chancellor of the English monarch, he was "preceded by two hundred and fifty boys on foot, in groups of six, ten, or more together, singing English songs, according to the custom of their country."[2]

We have but to look in Chaucer's "Canterbury Tales" to see how that the knowledge of music, and the love of song, pervaded all classes. Of the Squire he says that—

"Syngynge he was, or flewtynge (fluting) al the day."

And that—

"He cowde songes wel make and endite."

Mr. Chappell well sums up what we learn from Chaucer relative to the musical knowledge of his day.

"We learn," he says, "from the preceding quotations, that country squires in the fourteenth century could pass the day in singing or playing the flute; that the most attractive accomplishment in a young lady was to be able to sing well, and that it afforded the best chance of her obtaining an eligible husband; also that the cultivation of music extended to every class. The miller, of whose education Pierce Plowman speaks so slightingly, could play upon the bagpipe; and the apprentice both on the ribble and gittern."[3]

The knights as they rode to tourney or on an embassy sang ballads. So, in the Romance of Florence of Rome—

"Thorow the towne the knyghtes sange,
And ever ther bryght brydyls range,
Making swete mynstralcy."

It was indeed part of the training of a perfect knight to be a musician. In the Romance of Sir Degrevaunt, in the Thornton collection, published by the Camden Society, we are told of the hero—

"He was ffayre mane and ffree,
And gretlech yaff (gave) him to gle,
To harp and to sautré,
And geterne ffull gay,
Well to play on a rote,
Of Lewtyng, welle y wote,
And syngyng many suet not (sweet note),
He bare the pryse aye."

---

[1] "Hist. of Music," ii. 553.   [2] Fitz-Stephen, *Vita S. Thomæ Cant.*   [3] "Popular Music of the Olden Time," 1st ed., p. 35.

Here, then, the same man is master of five instruments—harp, psaltery, cithern, rote, and lute—besides being able to sing; no doubt he sang and accompanied himself on one of these stringed instruments.

No banquet was complete without music. So, in the Romance of Octavian—

> "Ther myghth men here menstralcye,
> Trompys, taborus, and cornettys crye,
> Roowte, gyterne, lute, and sawtrye,
> Fydelys, and othyr mo."

It was a token of the direst distress, when no music was heard at a meal. In Florence of Rome, the Emperor says, when girt in by his foes, and hopeless of rescue—

> "Of mynstralcy we kepe none,
> We have no space to spare;
> Nodeor harpe, fedyll, nor geest."

The "gest" is the long ballad of heroic deeds that was sung to the accompaniment of the harp. Perhaps the absence of fiddle, as well as of harp, denoted that in the palace there was neither "carping" (singing) nor dancing.

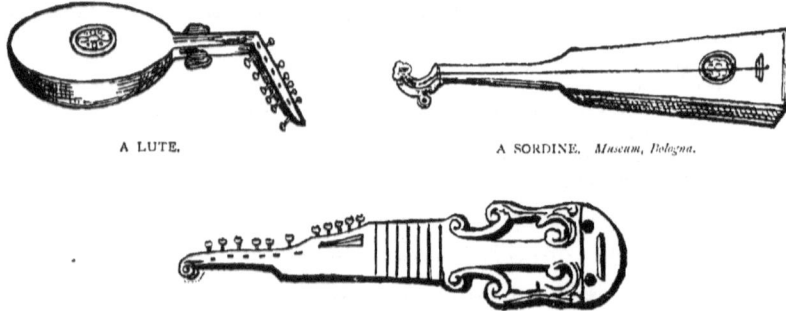

A LUTE.

A SORDINE. *Museum, Bologna.*

PSALTERY. *Museum, Bologna.*

There were, in fact, songs adapted to the several instruments by which they were accompanied, that is to say, the character of the melody was such as suited various kinds of accompaniments.

Thus Wace, in his account of the coronation feast of King Arthur, is careful not only to enumerate the various musical instruments that were played thereat, but also the kinds of songs that were sung with them. I will give the translation of the Norman French.

"Many *jonglers* were there at the court, singers, and rhymers; many songs might you hear, Rote-songs, and vocal-songs; fiddlers' lays and notes; lays for fiddles, lays for rotes; lays for harps, lays for pipes (*fietalx*); lyres and panpipes (*chalemealx*); symphonies, psalteries, monochords, cymbals, chorus. There were enough of conjurers (*tregetours*), of male and female performers; some told tales and fables."

Erasmus, speaking of the English, in the reign of Henry VIII., said that they challenged the prerogative of having the handsomest women, of keeping the best table, and of being the most accomplished in music of any people. When Thomas Cromwell, Earl of Essex, went to Rome in 1510, he gave a three-part English song before Pope Julius II., to the surprise and delight of the Pontiff, to whom part-singing was a novelty.

These three part-songs were called "Freemen's" songs, and we happily have Ravenscroft's collections of some that were sung in the court of Henry VIII. in those most precious and interesting volumes, "Pammelia," 1609, "Deuteromelia," 1609, and "Melismata," 1611. "Ravenscroft may perhaps be described as our first musical antiquary . . . his first publications, undertaken in 1609, when he was but seventeen years old, were an attempt to preserve popular music of the earlier part of the preceding century from the final oblivion which seemed to threaten it. We must be grateful, though we may wish he had done more to rescue it from the corruption into which it had fallen, and must often suspect that he is unwittingly misleading us."[1]

In the reign of Elizabeth, music was in universal estimation. "Not only was it a necessary qualification for ladies and gentlemen, but even the city of London advertised the musical abilities of boys educated in Bridewell and Christ's Hospital, as a mode of recommending them as servants, apprentices, or husbandmen. In Delaney's 'History of the Gentle Craft,' 1598, one who tried to pass as a shoemaker was detected as an impostor, because he could neither 'sing, sound the trumpet, play upon the flute, nor reckon up his tools in rhyme.' Tinkers sang catches; milkmaids sang ballads; cadgers whistled; each trade, and even the beggars, had their special songs; the bass-viol hung in the drawing-room for the amusement of waiting visitors; and the lute, cittern, and virginals, for the amusement of waiting customers, were the necessary furniture of a barber's shop. They had music at dinner; music at supper; music at weddings; music at funerals; music at night; music at dawn; music at work; and music at play."[2]

If we stride on to the end of the seventeenth century, we find that notwithstanding the terrible extinguisher of the Puritan domination, music was as dear to English hearts, and as generally cultivated, as three hundred years before.

Pepys' Diary gives evidence to this. His household included a maid to wait upon his wife, and a boy to attend upon himself. In the course of his diary four maids are mentioned, and all possessed of some skill in music. Of the first he says (Nov. 17, 1662): "After dinner, talking with my wife, and making Mrs. Gosnell sing. . . . I am mightily pleased with her humour and singing." And on Dec. 5: "She sings exceedingly well." Within a few months, Gosnell was succeeded by Mary Ashwell, who could play on the "harpsichon," and he bought a Verginal book, from which she might play. Of a third servant, Mercer, he writes on Sept. 9, 1664: "After dinner, my wife and Mercer, Tom (the boy) and I, sat till eleven at night, singing and fiddling, and a great joy it is to see me master of so much pleasure in my house. The girl (Mercer) plays pretty well upon the harpsichon, but only ordinary tunes, but hath a good hand, sings a little, but hath a good voyce and eare. My boy, a brave boy, sings finely, and is the most pleasant boy at present, while his ignorant boy's tricks last, that ever I saw." Mercer left; then, in October 1666, Pepys writes: "My wife came home and hath brought her newe girle I helped her to. . . . Her voice, for want of use, is so furred that it does not at present please me; but her manner of singing is such, that I shall, I think, take great pleasure in it."

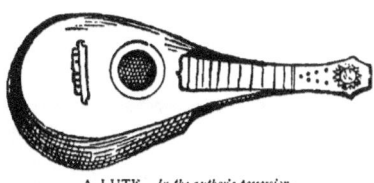

A LUTE. *In the author's possession.*

On Dec. 26, 1668, Pepys writes: "After supper I made the boy play upon his lute."

In the country, music was as dearly loved as in towns.

Dorothy Osborne, in one of her charming letters to Sir William Temple, writes, in 1653: "The heat of the day is spent in reading or working, and about six or seven o'clock I walk out into a common that lies hard by the house, where a great many young wenches keep sheep and cows, and sit in the shade singing of ballads. I go to them and compare their voices and beauties to some ancient shepherdesses that I have read of, and find a vast difference there; but trust me, I think these are as innocent as those could be. I talk to them, and find they want nothing to make them the happiest people in the world but the knowledge that they are so."

Oh! that Dorothy had but taken down these ballads and their accompanying melodies!

In Sir Thomas Overbury's "Character of a Milkmaid" he says: "She dares go alone, and enfold her sheep in the night, and fears no manner of ill, because she means none; yet, to say truth, she is never alone, she is still accompanied with old songs, honest thoughts, and prayers, but short ones."

We must now turn from consideration of English love of music to the history of secular music, specially of song.

A word or two must needs be said relative to the minstrels, the so to speak musical college of the Middle Ages. With them probably originated most of the ballad airs. But they were players on many instruments; some formed a local guild, and sat in the screen dividing the chancel from the nave of the church, and accompanied divine worship with their instrumental music. Such minstrels are represented at the east end of Launceston parish church, carved in granite. At Beverley minster also the minstrels are represented.

There is a curious story characteristic of the Middle Ages told of the illustrious family of Crussol, that obtained the Dukedom of Uzès. There were, in the early part of the thirteenth century, three brothers living on a little estate in a ruinous castle at Uzès, near Nimes. They were all three unmarried and in very pinched circumstances. So one day

[1] H. Ellis Wooldridge, Int. to Chappel, 2nd ed., *op. cit.*   [2] *Op. cit.*, new ed., p. 59.

the eldest, Ebles, said to his brothers that it was a shabby life for three gentlemen thus to live, or stagnate, in their poverty. Let them all three leave the crumbling walls and leaky roof of Uzès, and seek their fortune in the courts of princes. His advice was relished, and they invited their cousin Elias, great in broad comedy, to travel with them. Now Guy, the youngest of the brothers, and Ebles the eldest, had a pretty gift at poetry, and the second brother, Pierre, had a pleasant pipe, so they agreed that Ebles and Guy should write songs and ballads, and that Pierre should sing them, whilst they would twang the *rote* in accompaniment. The profits of the little company were to be equally divided among them. The brothers and cousin had great success with their songs wherever they went, and realised a capital wherewith they were able to restore the fortunes of the family, which after that looked up in the world, and became one of the most powerful in the south.

Minstrels wandered about the country. In the Romance of Sir Cleges, such are shown travelling to the court of Uthyr Pendragon at Cardiff. Sir Cleges—

> " - — as he walkyd upp and doun
> Sore syghthyng, he heard a soune
> Of dyvers mynstrelsee ;
> Of trompes, pypes, and claraneris,
> Of harpis, luttis, and getarnys,
> Of sotile, and sawtrè ;
> Many carellys, and gret daunsyng ;
> On every syde he hard syngyng,
> In every place trewly."

The minstrels fell out of favour in the reign of Henry VIII., and still more so in that of Elizabeth. Puttenham in his "Arte of English Poesie," 1589, speaks of "ballads and small popular musickes sung by canto-banqui upon benches and barrels' heads, where they have none other audiences than boyes or countrye fellowes that pass by them in the streete, or else by blind harpers, or such like tavern minstrels that give you a fit of mirth for a groat, and their matter being for the most part stories of old time, as the tale of Sir Topas, Bevis of Southampton, Guy of Warwick, Adam Bell, and Clym of the Clough, and such other old romances or historical rhymes, made purposely for the recreation of the common people at Christmas dinners and bridales, and in taverns and such other places of base resort."

In 1593 an Act was passed putting down minstrels, and it was ordered that any one caught wandering from place to place, with minstrelsy as his profession, was to be treated as a rogue and a vagabond.

The itinerant ballad-singer was indeed degenerate, if we may judge by W. Browne, who thus speaks of him in his "Britannia's Pastorals" in 1616—

From a Broadside.

> "As ballad-mongers on a market day,
> Taking their stands, one (with as harsh a noise
> As ever cart-wheele made) squeales the sad choice
> Of Tom the Miller with the Golden Thumb.
> .   .   .   .   .
> Half-part he chants, and will not sing it out."

The third Parliament of Cromwell again smote the minstrels, not now for travelling about, but for frequenting taverns. It was enacted that any minstrel or ballad-singer caught singing or making music in an ale-house, or was found to have solicited any one to hear him sing and play, was to be taken before the first magistrate, whipped, and imprisoned. In 1642 it was gravely proposed in Parliament, seeing the popularity of ballads and of carols, that the great deeds of Oliver Cromwell should be put into rhyme, and set to be sung at Christmas, in lieu of the carols in honour of Christ's Nativity, so dear to the hearts of the English people. The proposal was not favoured, and nothing came of it. On Dec. 13, 1648, there was a Provost-Marshal appointed, "with powers to seize upon all ballad-singers, and to suppress stage-plays."

But the Rebellion struck and injured not merely the ballad-minstrels, it affected all instrumentalists attached to theatres and churches, and led to a great migration of our musicians to the Continent.

AN HISTORICAL SKETCH OF ENGLISH NATIONAL SONG

The character of English, and, indeed, of all early melodies depends very much on the instrument to which they were sung. There were harp and lute accompaniments to ballads, and many a ballad air seems to call out for the stringed instrument to fill up the background. In "Songs of the West," I have given one or two of these traditional harp airs; all the Welsh melodies proclaim that they were composed to be chanted by a minstrel who was attended by a harpist. So do many of those in the West of England. "The Three Sisters," given by Gilbert in his "Cornish Carrols," is distinctly a harp air. The harp was played in England in the seventeenth century. M. Jorevin de Rochefort, who printed his travels in England in 1672, says: "The harp was then the most esteemed of musical instruments by the English." Carew, in his Survey of Cornwall, 1607, speaking of Tregarrick, then the residence of Mr. Butler, the sheriff, tells how that the house had belonged to the Wideslades, who had been dispossessed because of their adherence to the Roman

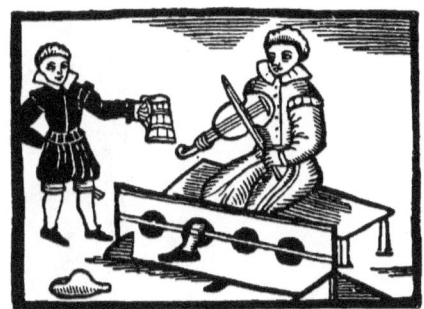

From a Broadside.

From a Broadside.

Catholic religion, and the "son then led a walking life, with his harp, to gentlemen's houses, where-through, and by his other active qualities, he was entitled Sir Tristram; neither wanted he (as some say) a *belle Isound*, the more aptly to resemble his pattern."

In the "Pleasant, plain, and pithy Pathway leading to a virtuous life," written about 1550, the author says:—

> "Very lusty I was, and pleasant withall
> To sing, dance, and play at the ball. . . .
> And besides all this, I could then finely play
> On the harp, much better than now far away,
> By which my minstrelsy and my fair speech and sport,
> All the maids in the parish to me did resort."

In Laneham's Letter, descriptive of the revelries at Kenilworth in 1575, he describes the minstrel with his harp, who sang a gest of King Arthur.

We are accustomed, nowadays, to associate the bagpipe with Scotland alone, but the bagpipe was of universal occurrence in Europe, and Scotland is merely the last refuge to which it has retired. Not only do a large number of airs show that they were composed to the drone of the bagpipe, but we have positive evidence that this instrument was in use, by its representation in carving of wood and stone. At Aruns, in the Pyrenees, is a white marble font on which

COUNTRY DANCE. *From a Font, Aruns.*

is represented a country dance, and a piper—looking for all the world as if kilted—is performing on what is now considered to be the peculiar instrument of the Highlands of Scotland.

At Altarnun, in Cornwall, a carved oak bench end, of about 1525, represents a bagpipe player with his dog, whilst a fiddler is sculptured on another. Among the minstrels carved on the outside of Launceston church is one with a

AN HISTORICAL SKETCH OF ENGLISH NATIONAL SONG

bagpipe; and in Sutton Place, near Guildford, the old seat of the Westerns, is a quarry in the hall whereon is figured a goose playing a bagpipe. This is of the date 1520, and gives indication that the bagpipe was falling into ridicule. An old sow playing on this instrument to the delectation of its piglings, is a not infrequent subject on Perpendicular bosses to vaulting-ribs.

For dances, tabor and pipe were favourite instruments; and there are tunes that imply such an accompaniment. I have given one in "The Garland of Country Song." The custom was, in England, for dancers to sing a ballad, and the different turns of the tune, or recurrence of the burden, marked the different movements in the dance. To this day, ballet signifies a dance, and ballad a song—the names bear trace of the early union between singing and dancing.

BENCHEND. *Altarnun.*

STAINED GLASS. *Sutton Place.*

CORNISH PIPER.
Knife handle found near Lostwithiel,
17th century.

Tabor and pipe were in use in villages, and probably formed all the instrumental music for the out-of-door dances, from May to Michaelmas. Misson, who travelled in England in the reign of James II. and William III., describes the dances of milkmaids to the bagpipes.

In an old song picked up in the West of England, these were the music of the haysel dance, together with the viol-di-gamba.

"The pipe and tabor both shall play,
The viols loudly ring,
From morn till eve each summer day,
As we go hay-making."

In Drayton's "Poly-olbion," 1613, a list is given of the musical instruments in common use in England. After mentioning viol, viol-di-gamba, cithern, pandore, theorbo, gittern and kit "the wandering fiddler's echo," cornet, fife, hautboi, sackbut, recorder, flute, shalm, cornamuse, he adds—

"Some blew the Bag-pipe up, that plays the Country-Round,
The Tabor and the Pipe some take delight to sound."

Even so late as Dibdin's time these two instruments seem to have been in use in country places.

The hornpipe was in use from a much earlier age than is usually imagined. We are so accustomed to associate it with nautical airs, and so disposed to believe that most, if not all, these latter belong to the Dibdin period, that it is with some surprise that we read of the hornpipe in Carew's "Survey of Cornwall," as having been much in use in that part of England in the reign of Henry VIII. But, indeed, the hornpipe figures in sculpture of a much earlier age. It was a pipe of hollow wood, with holes for the fingers at intervals, and with a horn mouthpiece, and a horn ring at the larger end.

Chaucer mentions it as a Cornish instrument—

> "Controve he would, and foule faile,
> With Hornpipes of Cornwale."

In the sixteenth and seventeenth centuries, the counties most famous for the hornpipe were Derbyshire, Nottinghamshire, and Lancashire. A common broadside ballad illustration of this period represents a female ballad-singer attended by a man who plays on the hornpipe.

HORNPIPE. *From a Garland.*

BALLAD-SINGER, AND HORNPIPE. *From a Broadside.*

There can be little mistake as to which tunes belong to this instrument. That, for instance, to which the "Furry dance" is performed annually at Helstone, in Cornwall, is a hornpipe.

The lute much resembled a guitar, but was a nobler instrument. The "Merry Monarch" was a great admirer of the instrument, and it was a favourite with all lovers in the Stuart age. Yet Dr. Burney, in his "History of Music" (iii. p. 143), says: "The lute, of which hardly the sound or shape is known at present, was during the last two centuries the favourite chamber instrument of every nation in Europe." It was driven out by the spinet and harpsichord, which afforded an easy path to those musical ends which had previously been reached through the lute, only after much difficulty and labour.

LUTE. *From the Museum, Bologna.*

One of our early English poets, Sir Thomas Wyatt (1503-1542), has left us some charming verses under the title, "The Lover's Lute cannot be blamed though it sing of his Lady's unkindness." The first lines run:—

> "Blame not my Lute! for he must sound
> Of this or that as liketh me;
> For lack of Wit the Lute is bound
> To give such Tunes as pleaseth me;
> Though my Songs be somewhat strange,
> And speak such Words as touch my Change,
> Blame not my Lute!"

Thomas Mace, in his "Musick's Monument" (1676), gives instructions how to preserve a lute in order. "Know," says it, "that an old lute is better than a new one . . . you shall do well, even when you lay it by in the day-time, to put it into a bed that is constantly used, between the rug and the blanket; but never between the sheets, because they may be moist . . . only no person must be so inconsiderate as to tumble down upon the bed whilst the lute is there, for I have known several good lutes spoilt with such a trick."

Formerly, in Devonshire, every farm-house had an instrument called the thrums, hung in the common hall; it consisted of a board with fret and strings, and was taken in the evening by one of the farmer's sons or daughters, or by one of the farm labourers, and he or she struck chords on it whilst singing a ballad.

In English country places, a groat for "a fit of mirth" was long the fee of the itinerant musician; and every villager, male or female, gave twopence for a dance on the green.

The fiddle is an instrument of English origin, it is the Anglo-Saxon fithele. It had in earliest times four strings only, and the neck was far shorter than at present. Another name for the fiddle is a crowd. In one of the sculptures on the outside of St. John's Church, Cirencester, is a player on a fiddle with a neck of well-proportioned length. The date of this carving is between 1504 and 1522, but from a representation of a "crowder" on a bench end at Altarnun Church, Cornwall, of much the same date, we see that the fiddle neck was also still sometimes quite short. This is the "kit," or fiddle used for dances.

A CROWDER.
From Benchend, Altarnun.

The fiddle supplanted tabor and pipe in last century, for dance music; and the sole representative of the ancient minstrel was the village fiddler.

The fiddle exercised great influence in the alteration and corruption of dance and ballad tunes, owing to the facility with which the instrument lent itself to the multiplication of notes, and to runs. Moreover, the fiddle banished the ballad as a song accompaniment to a dance. Nevertheless, as a very aged fiddler told me that, in his early days, the lads and maids always sang whilst dancing to his music. Nearly all our oldest country dances are named after the ballads to which they were sung.

From a Broadside Ballad.

Sir Thomas Elyot, in his "Governor," 1531, after describing the ancient modes of dancing, says: "And as for the special names (of the dances), they were taken, as they be now, either of the names of the first inventors, or of the measure and number they do contain; or, of the *first words of the ditty which the song comprehendeth, whereof the dance was made.*"

I annex a list of the dances given by Playford in the first edition (1651) of his English Dancing-master; the names tell their own tale:—

1. Upon a summer's day. (*)
2. Blew Cap. (*)
3. The Night piece, or, The Shaking of the Sheets. (*)
4. The Boate-man, a Bagpipe tune, with drone.
5. The Beggar boy. (*)
6. The Parson's Farewell.
7. Bobbing Joe (Joan?) "My dog and I" is sung to this.
8. The New Exchange.
9. The Wish.
10. Stingo, or, Oyle of Barley. (*)
11. The Whirligig.
12. Picking of Sticks.
13. The Old Mole.
14. Grimstock.
15. Woodicock.
16. Greenwood. This is "Shall I go walk the Woods so wild?" (*)
17. A Saraband.
18. Hit and Misse.
19. Confesse, or, The Court Lady. (*)
20. A Health to Betty.
21. Mage on a Tree.
22. Millison's (Milicent's) Jegge.
23. The Spanish Jeepsie (Gipsy). This is "Come follow, follow me." (*)
24. Lady Spillor.
25. Kemp's Jegg (called after Nine Days' Wonder Kemp).
26. If all the world were paper. (*)
27. The Chirping of the Larke. This is Robin Hood and Guy of Gisborne. (*)
28. Adson's Saraband.
29. None such, or, A la mòde de France. (*)
30. The merry, merry Milkmaids. (*)
31. Daphne. "When Daphe did from Phœbus fly." (*)
32. Mill-field (*)
33. The fine Companion.
34. Cast a bell.
35. Shellamefago.
36. The Rose is red, and the Rose is white.
37. The Spanyard.
38. Have at thy coat, old Woman. (*)
39. To Drive the Cold Winter away, or, The Gun. (*)
40. Pepper's Black.
41. The Maid Peept out at the Window, or, The Friar in the Well. (*)
42. Halfe Hanniken.
43. Once I loved a maiden faire. (*)
44. Faine I would, or, "The King's Complaint." (*)
45. The Irish Lady, or, Anniseed water Robin.
46. My Lady Cullen.
47. The Bath.
48. Jog on my Honey.
49. Goddesses. "I would I were in my own country." (*)
50. The Health, or, The Merry Weasel. (*)

51. Heart's Ease.
52. Jack Pudding.
53. Prince Rupert's March.
54. Dissembling Love, or, The Lost Heart.
55. Argeers
56. Jack-a-Lent.
57. Mayden Lane. (*?)
58. The Chirping of the Nightingale.
59. A Soldier's Life. (*)
60. Sweet Masters.
61. Cuckolds all a row, also the Cavalier's song, "Hey boys up we go." (*)
62. Petticoat Wag.
63. Paul's Steeple or, "I am the Duke of Norfolk." (*)
64. Rufty Tufty.
65. All in a garden green. (*)
66. Dargesson, or Sedanny, "The Hawthorn Tree." (*)
67. Aye Me!
68. The Punk's Delight.
69. The Milkmaydes Bobb.
70. An old Man is a Bedfull of bones. (*?)
71. Cheerily and Merrily.
72. The Country Coll.
73. Dull Sir John.
74. Saturday Night and Sunday Morning.
75. New Boe Peep. (*)
76. Hockley in the Hole.
77. The Chestnut.
78. Stanes Morris.
79. Paul's Wharfe.
80. Tom Tinker's my true Love. (*)
81. Kettle Drum, or, He that hath a good Wife.
82. Hide Parke.
83. Mundesse.
84. Ladye lye neare me. (*)
85. Lull me beyond thee. (*)
86. Jenny pluck Pears.
87. The Glory of the West. (*)
88. Gathering Peascods.
89. Scotch Cap.
90. New new Nothing.
91. Step Stately.
92. Shepherd's Holyday, or Labour in Vaine.
93. Graies Inn Maske.
94. The Slip.
95. The tender Gentlewoman, or, The Hemp-dressers.

I have marked with an asterisk those country dances of which the ballad words remain. There are several of the others to which later words have been set, that have displaced the original words.

I give this list at some length as showing how that collections of dance tunes have been the means of preserving to us a large number of ballad airs. But there were many other airs that would not lend themselves to dances. Very happily the ballad operas have been the means of saving these.

We must now consider an immense change which came over music in Europe, and a divorce which was effected between the music of the cultured and that of the people. This was produced by the introduction of *Time* as an element essential to music. In mediæval music there was no time, every note was lengthened or shortened according to the syllables to which it was attached. Song was the musical rendering of words. To the present day, Gregorian music is unbarred, whether for psalm or for hymn. We have but to look at a Gregorian hymn-melody as given, say, in Helmore's "Hymnal Noted," and the same as chopped up and put into strict modern tune in "Hymns Ancient and Modern," to see the difference. One of these magnificent old airs is like Pegasus in plough-harness when reduced to modern time in the latter Collection, where it is hardly recognisable in its degradation. All ballad airs were the same. But time of some kind was necessary in dancing, that was obvious, and the dance taught the musician what otherwise he might never have learned,—the use of *time*.

Having made this discovery, he found that it led to the most surprising results. He could write part-music without keeping each part exactly together, or counter-point, proper—point against point, or one note under another.

The musicians having discovered what could be done with part-singing if all performers kept time—a great discovery, with immense possibilities not for the voice only, but for instruments as well—at once began to abuse the knowledge they had acquired.

I must, however, note here the remarkable tenacity with which old English peasant singers cling to the natural system, and reject the artificial. They now sing strictly according to the sense of their words, and entirely ignore *time*, so that in taking down one of their airs it is often not possible to say in what time it is, whether in common or in triple measure.

So on the boards, a professional artist when he comes to sing a ballad, breaks through the bars, and follows the rhythm, regardless of time, and the accompanist has to attend to him. Unless they do this, ballad-singing is mechanical and devoid of attraction. It will charm nobody, and never provoke an encore.

The old minstrel airs were accompanied by stringed instruments, such as the crowd, which was flat bridged, so that when the bow was drawn across it, a succession of chords was the result. It had six strings, but of these two were drones, or *bourdons*, whose pitch was only altered when tuned; but the other four admitted of every variety of intonation possible without "shifting" the hand. There were other instruments, such as the psaltery, played without a bow, with the fingers, which we may say with certainty were so played to form an accompaniment in chords to the voice. The ballad air owed its charm to the melody, it could be sung without accompaniment or sung with it.

But when in the sixteenth century the science of part-singing began to be understood, then the musical composers,

AN HISTORICAL SKETCH OF ENGLISH NATIONAL SONG

in their delight at having this new field for their ingenuity open to them, turned away with scorn from the ballad air, and indeed from melody altogether, and endeavoured to compose pieces exhibiting the utmost possible ingenuity of structure on scientific principles wholly independent of air, and in supreme indifference whether or not the compositions were pleasing and taking to the ear. Tallis, as is well known, produced a *tour de force* in writing a song of forty parts. The first subject is begun in G by the first mezzo soprano; the second medius in like manner beginning in G, is answered by the first tenor in the octave below, and that by the first counter-tenor in D, the fifth above; then the first bass has the subject in D, the eighth below the counter-tenor; and thus the forty real parts are severally introduced in the course of thirty-nine bars, when the whole phalanx is employed at once during six bars more; after which, a new subject is led off by the lowest bass, and pursued by the other parts, severally, for about twenty-four bars, when there is another general chorus of all the parts; and thus this stupendous specimen of human labour and wrongheaded ingenuity is carried on in alternate flight, pursuit, attack, and choral union to the end, when it is concluded by twelve bars of universal chorus, in fortifold harmony. It was thought equally ingenious to take three or four independent airs—folk-airs as often as not—and work them together in and out into a structure that was ingenious and showed the skill of the composer, but could give pleasure to nobody. To such an extent was this the fashion, that among the Italian composers, when writing Masses, they took a wicked delight in weaving in the most inappropriate airs and sometimes those associated with obscene words into the sacred service, retaining the Latin words of *Gloria, Benedictus,* or *Agnus Dei,* for the tenor alone, and allowing the other parts to be sung to the original indecent Italian ballad words. Musical art was mechanical; there was no reason whatever why a man with a mathematical head should not compose a masterpiece, when he had grasped the fundamental laws of counterpoint, even though he could not tell by ear one tune from another.

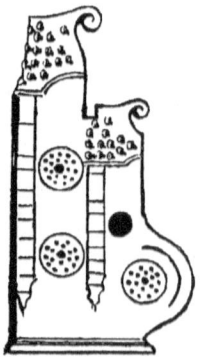

PSALTERY. *Museum, Bologna.*

One of the results of this fashion was that the musicians of the period were paralysed in all that concerned melody. There is hardly an instance to be discovered among their works of a composition built on an original theme, they felt about and laid hold of such airs, and scraps of airs, as were already to hand, and built these into their fabrics. This period produced one thing that was worth preservation—the madrigal, which sprang into life in England and in Italy simultaneously, and lasted from 1530 to 1630.

Meanwhile, in spite of the scorn poured on them by the scientific musician, the ballad-singers with their fresh delicious folk-airs—fresh yet old, but old assuming fresh characters—held the ear of the people, and for a dance, the exigencies of the case demanded a currant melody with a rhythmic time and harmonic base. In the tapestried galleries, in the panelled halls of the manor houses, the gentles and ladies in lace and velvet laboured at contrapuntal pieces, and believed that they had derived some pleasure from having been able to execute difficult passages; but on the village green, in the ale-house, the country people held tenaciously to the traditions of pure melody.

Then came the Civil War and the domination of the Puritans, when the scientific musicians were scattered everywhere. The people did not miss them, they had never cared for their motetts and madrigals; and if the minstrel and the fiddler were suppressed by Act of Parliament, no Act of Parliament could restrain the mother from singing to her babe, the milkmaid from warbling under the cow, the old ballads they loved so well to the dear old tunes that they had themselves learned in infancy.

At the Restoration, such musicians as were still alive were drawn from their retreats, and placed in positions where they might train up a new generation, and carry on the old traditions of English music. But they found themselves in a new world, not one that would longer tolerate their tediousness, and listen to their consequential affectation. The new world would have no more of this; it must have song—pure melody—and the orchestra was becoming a power which these relics of the age of motette and madrigal did not understand. They sneered at Charles II. with his "four and twenty fiddlers all of a row," but the fiddlers carried the day. The old masters of music, Child, Christopher Gibbons, and Low had to retire, and a new generation took their places, who had been taught at the feet of Lulli in Paris.

Pelham Humphrey was sent by Charles II. to be instructed by Lulli, and Humphrey was the master of Purcell.

Elaborate counterpoint, with all the intricacy of fugue, was just endurable in ecclesiastical music, but was insupportable in opera, and the opera now rose to be a dominating power in altering and moulding the character of music, and the nursery of the opera was Italy. But even there at first the composers followed a line that was not frankly popular. They elaborated the recitative, the *aria* was an after product. It was not so in Paris. Lulli had more sense, he had his finger on the pulse of the French people, and he cared nothing for his art save how it could make that pulse throb and leap as he listed. The people had no desire to have the "Prose" of the sanctuary transferred to the boards.

It was the same in England. There it was long before recitative in English found admission. Melody the English ear would have, and therefore melody had to be provided.

Intricate and scientifically constructed music may be interesting, as a puzzle of any sort interests, but it cannot please. It is a manifestation of the composer's skill, not of his genius. Any one properly trained, and with a mathematical head, could write a fugue, but only a musically-gifted soul can evolve an air. Elaborate contrapuntal music resembles verses in which there is strict accuracy in the metre, and in the rhyme, but that is all. A pure melody is like a poetic thought, the spirit of life which alone can animate the dry bones of theoretical music. Kelly, in his Reminiscences, says: "I may safely aver, from my own knowledge, that I have met with ninety-nine good theorists to one melodist; nature makes one, study the other. Two of the greatest theorists that I ever met with were, Padre Martini of Bologna, and Sala, Master of the Conservatorio, Naples; yet neither of these ever produced a remarkable melody that I recollect; I mean, not such an one as our justly celebrated composer, Dr. Arne, used to say, 'would grind about the streets upon an organ.'"

Haydn said of melody, "It is the air which is the charm of music, and it is that which is most difficult to produce. Patience and study are sufficient for the composition of agreeable sounds, but the invention of a fine melody is the work of genius; the truth is, a fine air needs neither ornament nor accessories in order to please,—would you know whether it really be fine, sing it without accompaniments." The opinion of Mozart was the same. Kelly records a conversation he had with him on the subject. "Melody is the essence of music," said Mozart, "*I* compare a good melody to a fine racer, and counterpointists to hack post-horses."

The first great composer of the new school was Purcell, a musical genius of the highest order; and he exhibited his genius by the creation of splendid melodies. Unhappily in many instances he yielded to the corrupt taste of the times, in sacrificing melody to supposed exigencies of the text.

Purcell died young, in 1695, but for some years after his death his compositions were the chief music heard in England. He may be looked upon as the father of our national music apart from the ballad. In compositions for the theatre, though the colouring and effects of an orchestra were then but little known, yet he employed more than his predecessors, and gave to the voice a melody more interesting than had been allowed by the scholarly numskulls of the past in this country, even, perhaps, in Italy, and he became the darling and delight of the nation. The only man at all on his level in Europe at the time was Corelli, but none of his music was printed and circulated till 1710, so that Purcell had no better Italian instrumental music to imitate than that of Bassini, Torelli, and others inferior to them. Yet his orchestration excels all these in fancy, modulation, and delicacy.

The first opera ever produced in England was written by Sir William Davenant, Shakespeare's godson, who liked to have it thought that he was his son. This was "The Siege of Rhodes," given in 1650, the music to which was composed by Lawes, Cook, and Matthew Lock.

Shakespeare had introduced songs into his plays, and other dramatists did the same,—Ben Jonson, Beaumont and Fletcher, Middleton, Dekker, and Webster; and these plays were the parents of the ballad-opera.

In "The Bloody Brother," 1640, there is not only a concerted drinking-song, but a scene, the song of the Woman of the Cellar, the Butler, the Cook, and the Pantler, intermixed with chorus; it is, moreover, from this same play that the exquisite song "Take, oh! take these lips away," is derived.

Now the opera as understood at first in England was no more than an increase in the number of songs and choruses introduced. Hitherto the songs had been written to well-known airs, only exceptionally had they fresh music composed for them. But now that the opera became manageable, with the knowledge of orchestration generally prevalent in Italy, France, Germany, and England, some of our composers began to write for the stage. Thus Matthew Lock produced his marvellous Macbeth music. Purcell wrote "The Prophetess," 1690, "King Arthur" in 1691, "The Faery Queen" in 1692, "Bonduca" in 1695; "The Northern Lass" was not produced till after his death in 1706.

As affecting English song I have to mention the opera in this article; but with the origin and history of the English opera, I shall deal at length and in detail in my second essay.

AN HISTORICAL SKETCH OF ENGLISH NATIONAL SONG

It seemed as though we were at the cradle of a national operatic school. But now appeared on the scene a rival candidate for favours, which unhappily succeeded in displacing and killing the English opera.

In 1707, the Italian opera of "Arsinoe" was performed in London, and met with vast success. This led to the translation into English of a number of Italian operas, and their performance.

"The next step," says Addison, in the *Spectator*, March 21, 1710-11, "was the introduction of Italian actors into our opera, who sung their parts in their own language at the same time that our countrymen performed theirs in our native tongue. The king or hero of the play generally spoke in Italian, and his slaves answered him in English: the lover frequently made his court, and gained the heart of his princess, in a language which she did not understand. . . . This was the state of the English stage for about three years. At length the audience grew tired of understanding half the opera, and therefore, to ease themselves entirely of the fatigue of thinking, have so ordered it at present that the whole opera is performed in an unknown tongue."

The influx of Italian music for a while paralysed the English composers. Even Addison did not venture to say boldly that our native music was the best. "I would allow the Italian opera," he said, "to lend our English musick as much as may grace and soften it, but never entirely to annihilate and destroy it."

For some time no music that was not Italian was considered tolerable, and Italian singers were the rage. Margareta de l'Espin made ten thousand pounds on the boards.

Pope sneered at the false admiration for the foreign music affected by the leaders of fashion. He calls the Italian opera—

> "A Harlot form, soft sliding by,
> With mincing step, small voice, and languid eye:
> *Foreign* her air, her robe's discordant pride,
> In patch-work fluttering, and her head aside:
> By singing Peers up-held on either hand,
> She tripp'd and laugh'd, too pretty much to stand;
> Cast on the prostrate Nine a scornful look,
> Then thus in quaint Recitativo spoke:
> *O cara! cara!* silence all that train:
> Joy to great Chaos! let Division reign:
> Chromatic tortures soon shall drive them hence,
> Break all their nerves, and fritter all their sense:
> One trill shall harmonise joy, grief, and rage,
> Wake the dull Church, and lull the ranting Stage,
> To the same notes thy sons shall hum, or snore,
> And all thy yawning daughters cry, *Encore!*"
>
> (*Dunciad*, iv.).

Now ensued one of the most extraordinary revulsions of fashion conceivable, the like of which is unique in the annals of music.

We have seen how that English melody had dethroned and driven into oblivion the old school of formal scientists. It now rose up again in revolt—this time against foreign music. The Italian opera was in full swing, and had silenced the English muse, when, in 1727, Gay wrote "The Beggar's Opera," of which all the songs but two or three were set to folk melodies, born in England. He offered it to Cibber at Drury Lane, and it was rejected by him with contempt. It was accepted by Rich, the manager of the theatre in Lincoln's Inn Fields, and produced on the 29th January 1727-8. The success of the piece was considered doubtful for the greatest part of the first act, and was not quite determined till Polly Peachum sang her pathetic appeal to her parents—

> "O ponder well, be not severe
> To save a wretched wife,
> For on the rope that hangs my dear
> Depends poor Polly's life,"

and this, to the air of "The Babes in the Wood," familiar to the entire audience from their nurseries. The effect was magical. The audience broke into a roar of applause, and the success of the play was established. The plot of the piece is of the poorest, but people were refreshed, and rejoiced again to hear the old familiar notes of the English muse. The author, according to Mace, got the entire receipts of four nights, amounting in the aggregate to

£693, 13s. 6d., whereas Rich, the manager, after the piece had been performed thirty-six times, had pocketed nearly £4000. It was well said that this play had made Rich *gay*, and Gay *rich*. But it had a further effect, it drew away

THE BEGGAR'S OPERA. *After Hogarth.*

the audience from the Italian opera, and, as the wags said, had made that indeed what the other was in name, the Beggar's opera.

"The Beggar's Opera" contains sixty-nine airs, of which I give a list :—

1. An old woman clothed in Gray.
2. The bonny gray-eyed Morn.
3. Cold and raw.
4. Why is your faithful Slave disdained?
5. Of all the simple things. (The Mouse-trap.)
6. What shall I do to shew.
7. Oh, London is a fine town.
8. Grim King of the Ghosts.
9. Jenny, where hast thou been?
10. Thomas, I can not.
11. A Soldier and a Sailor.
12. Now ponder well, ye parents dear.
13. Le printemps. (French air.)
14. Pretty Parrot.
15. Pray, fair one, be kind.
16. Over the Hills and far away.
17. Gin thou wert mine ain thing.
18. O the Broom.
19. Fill every glass.
20. March in Rinaldo.
21. Would you have a young Virgin. (Poor Robin's maggot.)
22. Cotillon.
23. All in a misty Morning.
24. When once I lay.
25. When first I lay siege to my Chloris.
26. Courtiers! Courtiers! think it no Harm.
27. A lovely Lass to a Friar came.
28. 'Twas when the Sea was roaring, &c.
29. The Sun had loos'd his weary Team, &c.
30. How happy are we.
31. Of noble race was Shenkin.
32. (Old air, the title forgotten by Gay.)
33. London Ladies.
34. All in the Downs.
35. Have you heard of a frolicksome Ditty?
36. Irish Trot.
37. (Old air, the name of which Gay had forgotten.)
38. Gossip Joan.
39. Irish Howl.
40. The Lass of Patie's Mill.
41. If Love's a sweet Passion.
42. South Sea Ballad.
43. Packington's Pound.
44. Lillibullero.
45. Down in the North Country.

AN HISTORICAL SKETCH OF ENGLISH NATIONAL SONG

46. A Shepherd kept Sheep.
47. One Evening passing lost my Way.
48. Now, Roger, I'll tell thee.
49. O Betsy Bell.
50. Would Fate to me.
51. Come sweet Lass.
52. The Last Time I went o'er the Moor.
53. Tom Tinker's my true Love.
54. I am a poor Shepherd undone.
55. Ianthe the lovely.
56. A Cobbler there was.
57. Bonny Dundee.
58. Happy Groves.
59. Sally in our Alley.
60. Britons strike home.
61. Chevy Chace.
62. Old Sir Simon the King.
63. Joy to Great Cæsar.
64. There was an old woman.
65. Did you ever hear of a gallant soldier.
66. Why are thine Eyes still glancing.
67. Green Sleeves.
68. All you that must take a leap.
69. Lumps of Pudding.

Gay was not himself anything of a musician. He had his head full of old songs and their airs, and he set to the latter songs suitable to his characters and the dialogue, then got a German named Pepusch to note them down for him,

VAUXHALL. *From the Headpiece of an Engraved Song.*

and write a simple orchestral accompaniment, and an overture. Owing to the success of the opera Pepusch republished all the airs arranged as catches, under the title of "The Agreeable Choice."

The enormous success of "The Beggar's Opera" encouraged others to follow in the same track. Indeed Gay himself repeated the same course in "Polly" and in "Achilles."

Over forty ballad operas appeared, and as most of these were published along with the music, they furnish us with a treasury of the folk-airs of the English people. In "The Beggar's Opera" were 69; in "The Generous Freemason" were 63; in "Achilles," 54; in "The Jovial Crew," 53; in "Momus turned Fabulist" there were 69, and there were 68 in "The Fashionable Lady."[1]

The immense success of "The Beggar's Opera" and its imitations served a purpose for which we cannot but be grateful, in addition to the debt we owe them of preserving for us a host of old English folk-airs. The English musicians were now encouraged to try their hands on original ballad operas; and we see many of these appear after the public taste for "The Beggar's Opera" had ceased.

The great Arne rose on the horizon, a man who followed the best traditions of good English music, who attempted to pick up the thread dropped by Purcell, and inaugurate English opera in contradistinction to the ballad opera, that is to say, an opera with musical recitatives, *aria parlante* as well as *aria cantibile*, and *scenas*. But the fashionables who patronised the theatre were not disposed to favour the undertaking, and Arne was obliged to fall back again on ballad operas. Then we have Arnold, Attwood, Storace, Shield, Kelly, Dibdin; and we reach another mighty name, that of Bishop. Next to whom comes Balfe, and then till the present no toleration of anything English, only Italian and German operas, and French light comic operas.

That which produced quite as much influence on the popular taste as the opera were the performances at Cupar's Gardens, Vauxhall, Ranelagh, Mary-le-bon—an influence quite as great, though not as debasing, as our modern music halls. The singers at the Gardens, male and female, became popular, and their songs were engraved in copperplate on half-sheets and circulated throughout England, or were collected into volumes, such as Worgan's "Agreeable Choice," or "Clio and Euterpe," and "Calliope."

Leveridge was a bass singer at the theatre in Lincoln's Inn Fields, but in 1726 he opened a coffee-house in Tavistock Street, Covent Garden, and published a collection of his songs in two pocket volumes, neatly engraved. To him English minstrelsy is indebted for the setting of Gay's "Black-Eyed Susan," and "The Roast Beef of Old England."

Worgan supplied Vauxhall with songs from 1753 to 1761, and after a break of connection, again from 1770 to 1774. His first book of Vauxhall songs was published in 1753. It is somewhat singular that one whose music was vastly popular should have left no song that has maintained a hold on the popular taste. Arne, Boyce, Greene, Carey, Festing, Gaillard, all wrote for the Gardens, where sang Mrs. Bracegirdle, Mrs. Clive, Miss Weichsell—afterwards Mrs. Billington —and Miss Stevenson, and among men, Beard, Lowe, Wilder. I shall have something to say of these singers in my Third Essay on the Gardens and Concert Halls.

The first engraving of music on metal plates was practised in England before any other country, and as early as the reign of James I. The two first music engravers were William and Robert Hole. After 1690 engraved half-sheets of music with songs became very common. Among the encomiastic verses on Dr. Blow, prefixed to his *Amphion Anglicus* in 1700, the poet says—

> "Long have we been with balladry oppress'd,
> Good sense lampoon'd, and harmony burlesqu'd:
> Whole reams of Single Songs became our curse,
> With bases wondrous lewed, and trebles worse.
> But still the luscious lore goes glibly down,
> And still the *double entendre* takes the town.
> They print the names of those who set and wrote 'em,
> With Lords at top and blockheads at the bottom."

It need hardly be said that these half-sheets of music are now highly valued, and are of great interest to the musical antiquary.

A great change had passed over English music. The influence of the Italian opera had not been unfelt, and had lightened it, and had made the composers think more of melody than of counterpoint. Charles II. had treated English music somewhat contemptuously. He cared not for very elaborate compositions, and liked only such music as he could beat time to.

The virginals, the spinet, and the harpsichord had displaced the lute, and songs were now written to the new instruments. Moreover English singers had acquired vocal gymnastics from the Italians, and the new songs were

---

[1] The following is an approximate list of the ballad operas:—1727, The Beggar's Opera; 1728, Polly, The Quaker's Opera, Penelope, The Village Opera, Love in a Riddle; 1729, Flora, or Hob in the Well, The Patron, Southwark Fair, The Cobbler's Opera, The Country Wedding, The Lover's Opera, The Wedding, The Beggar's Wedding, Damon and Phillida, Love and Revenge; 1730, Robin Hood, The Bayes' Opera; 1731, The Grub Street Opera, Silvia, The Generous Freemason, The Devil to pay, The Merry Cobbler, The Highland Fair; 1732, The Humours of the Court, The Disappointment, The Footman, The Court Legacy, The Female Parson, The Jovial Crew; 1733, Achilles, The Fancyd Queen, The Stage Mutineers, The Mad Captain, The Boarding School, The Livery Rake, The Devil of a Duke, The Mock Doctor, Lord Blunder's Confession, The Opera of Operas; 1734, Don Quixote in England, The Chambermaid, The Lottery, The Old Man taught Wisdom; 1735, The Honest Yorkshireman, The Intriguing Chambermaid; 1736 (none); 1737, The Rape of Hellen; 1739, Margery, Roger and Joan. The exact date cannot be fixed of The Sturdy Beggars, and Cure for a Cold. Some were printed, but never performed. Some were printed without the music, but with the names of the airs to which the songs were to be sung.

overladen with runs, trills, twirls, and divisions, that obscured the underlying melody, as a broidery of glass beads or spangles over silk brocade.

But the most significant change of all was that of abandonment of the old Gregorian modes for the modern mode. If we take a volume of D'Urfey's "Pills to Purge Melancholy," or even the "Beggar's Opera," we shall find how

PORTION OF A HALF-SHEET SONG. *Circ.* 1740.

unlike much of the music there is to anything which pleases nowadays. The English ear has lost the faculty of enjoying a minor air, has come to regard such as dolorous, yet it was in such modes and in minor keys that many of the old dance tunes were set, and the most boisterous Bacchanalian songs were sung.

Our faculty of appreciation has become narrowed. It may come that we shall in time extend our sympathy, and come to delight in melodies in other keys than those to which we will now tolerate all music.

Let us see in what this immense change consists.

In modern music we have two *scales* only, the major and the minor. By scale is meant the regular order in which successive sounds follow each other, ascending or descending. To these sounds we give the name of notes, and any note from which we commence our scale is said to be the key-note of the scale. In modern music, from whichever note we commence our scale the sounds must always follow in the same order, that is to say, with the semitones invariably in the same places, *i.e.*, falling between the 3rd and 4th sounds, or else, between the 2nd and 3rd; or to put the case in another form, there are only two sounds in a "natural" scale that we allow as key-notes, the first sound C, and the sixth A, and when a scale is constructed on the latter of these, then the notes of the scale have to be modified in two places to satisfy the modern ear.

THOMAS D'URFEY.

Now it is obvious that we may begin our scale anywhere in the octave, and by so doing vary the position of the semitone.

In the ancient scales, neither flats nor sharps had any existence, so that they could not thus modify a scale, and that on A would run thus—

In the scale of C, the half-tones occur between the 3rd and 4th notes, and between the 7th and 8th.
In the scale of D, between the 2nd and 3rd, and the 6th and 7th.
In the scale of F, between the 4th and 5th, and the 7th and 8th.
In the scale of G, between the 3rd and 4th, and the 6th and 7th.
In the scale of A, between the 2nd and 3rd, and the 5th and 6th.

The key of B was never used.[1]

These scales were distinguished by the name of some Grecian province—

The scale of D	was called the	Dorian mode.
,,	E	,,	Phrygian mode.
,,	F	,,	Lydian mode.
,,	G	,,	Myxolydian mode.
,,	A	,,	Æolian mode.
,,	C	,,	Ionian mode.

But it will be seen that in the Dorian and Æolian modes, the position of the semitones is the same, between the 3rd and 4th notes; and likewise with the Myxolydian and Ionian. Rejecting, then, the Æolian and Ionian as repetitions of two former scales, we have left four scales. But to this four scales four more were added, each of which commenced at the *fourth* note of the original scale. These new scales were termed *plagal*, and the original scales *authentic*. These were also distinguished as Hypo-Dorian, Hypo-Phrygian, &c.

The modern scale (the Ionian was of course one among these, but melodies were by no means confined to it. In ecclesiastical music it was studiously avoided. Zarlino, a theorist of the sixteenth century, speaks of it as "well adapted for dances; the greater number of these we hear now in Italy are set in this mode, whence it has come that some call it in our days '*Il modo lascivo.*'"

Nevertheless, he admits that some of the church composers of more recent times had used it. But this perhaps was due to their having taken a loose song as the theme for the mass or hymn which they composed on it. In the Madrigalian era, 1530-1630, the old modes were almost wholly employed. In church music, Adrian Batten, organist

---

[1] The original scales consisted of five notes, not eight, as with us. "An instrument of ten strings," such as David speaks of, was one with two complete scales.

of St. Paul's Cathedral, who died 1640-50, was the last writer who employed them. He wrote anthems and a service in the Dorian mode. He was expelled his office at the Rebellion, in 1637. When Charles II. came to the throne, and insisted on having his French fiddlers in church, there was no more question of ecclesiastical modes. The fashion was set the other way, and not only on the stage, but in the stalls of the cathedral, *il m do lascivo* reigned supreme. The old scales took refuge in the songs of the people, where they remain embedded to the present day, which songs, when exhumed by enthusiasts, polished and made presentable, are found to be gems. The last musician in England who made a stand for the modes and advocated their use, was Dr. Pepusch, in a treatise published in 1746.

Attached to the French expedition to Egypt in 1799 were several savants, whose function it was to record observations on the antiquities, natural history, &c., of the Nile Basin. Among these was a M. Villoteau, a musician, who was deputed to collect information relative to Oriental music. On reaching Cairo, he placed himself under an Arabian music-master, whose lessons consisted in teaching his pupil to sing certain airs by ear and from memory. M. Villoteau set to work to write out these melodies, and observing, as he wrote, that the intonation of the Arab singer was occasionally false, he took care to allow for his supposed inaccuracies, and to put on paper not exactly what he heard, but what he *supposed* his master desired to sing, but failed through inaccuracy of his organ. This operation ended, M. Villoteau proceeded to test practically the accuracy of his work, but the Arab stopped him in the middle of the first phrase, telling his pupil that he was singing out of tune. Then the Arab produced a lute of native facture, the fingerboard divided by frets according to the rules of the Arabian scale. The mystery was explained in a moment. An inspection of the instrument showed M. Villoteau that the very elements of the music with which he was familiar, and those of the music with which he desired to make acquaintance, were absolutely different. The intervals of the two scales were dissimilar, and the education of the European musician made it difficult for him to seize and appreciate Arabian melody and to execute it.

Precisely the same thing happens when we come to collect the folk-music of the English peasantry. They sing in the old modes that were abandoned in the reign of Charles II. What we are inclined to do is to alter what is sung when noting the tunes down, but if we do this we make a great mistake, we lose completely the character of their traditional music. Many a time have I been checked and corrected by an aged singer, as was M. Villoteau, when I have played on the piano, or sung after him one of the ballad airs he has taught me, because I have put my semitone in the wrong place. This was at first, ten years ago. Now I am wiser, I *expect* to find a song in a church mode, and am no more puzzled when I do, and inclined to believe that the singer is wrong.

If we look at Playford's "Dancing Master," D'Urfey's "Pills," or Gay's "The Beggar's Opera," we shall find that the popular music of the English people was composed in the old modes, and to this day, our country singers prefer an air in a Dorian or Myxolydian mode to any modern one in the commonly received mode. We consider an air in one of the Gregorian modes to be melancholy, but not so the singers. There is an old hedger who is a dear friend of mine—he can neither read nor write—and he says to me, "Now I'll sing you a pretty little tune as lively as you ever heard," and he will strike up something in the Hypo-Myxolydian scale.

The change that came over English music at the close of the seventeenth century was due to the narrowing of our ground, and to the abandonment of all other scales save *il modo lascivo*, and that was due to Charles II. and his French fiddlers and Italian singers.

One great musical name must not pass unmentioned in our review of English music, but it is that of a great man who really influenced English song very slightly. This was Handel. He left his indelible impress on sacred music; on English song, almost none at all. He composed, in secular music, for the cultured, and not for the popular taste. The style of his operatic music was Italian, and not at all to the popular liking; and, indeed, the whole system of the Italian opera was artificial and ephemeral. Some few of his songs have become standard among us, as "Love in thine Eyes sits Playing," and "Ruddier than the Cherry." Look at Arne. His melody is fresh and enduring to the present day, because thoroughly popular. "Blow, blow, thou Winter Wind," "Where the Bee Sucks," "Under the Greenwood Tree," "Rule Britannia." These are the songs that have carried on the traditions of really good English music.

Haydn was the father of modern music. His "My Mother bids me Bind my Hair" is essentially modern music. He is the father of the modern symphony, the modern quartette, and the modern orchestration. The father of the modern opera is Mozart. His contemporary was Cimarosa, whose masterpiece "Il Matrimonio" was brought out in 1792. It suffices to compare this with "La Nozze di Figaro" to see the difference between the old style and the new.

To return from these names to English opera is to come down with a run. There is a reason for this. English music had its tradition broken, its composers dispersed, and when music began to lift up its head among us once more, it was systematically despised and made a mock of. Something was done by Arnold, Dibdin, Storace, Shield, but the really great name at the head of the century is that of Bishop, who has enriched English song with imperishable melodies. But Bishop did absolutely nothing to found English opera. All he did was to set gems of song on fustian dialogue. But we have had others, in addition to the composers for the theatre, who have contributed to the song of England —Clifton, Hudson, Blewitt—but they did nothing to improve the quality of our music. They mostly picked up folk-airs, altered them, modernised their key, and set them to vulgar ditties. I will conclude this notice of modern English music with the words of my friend and fellow-worker, the Rev. H. Fleetwood Sheppard:—

"After 1810, Bishop took and kept the lead, and did much for English song. His round, 'When the Wind blows then the Mill goes,' in 'The Miller and his Men,' is always popular now, and his name is inseparably connected with English music. Moore's songs, Irish chiefly,[1] filled up a void. Then came Knight with 'She wore a Wreath of Roses,' &c., whose songs were all the rage, and Crouch with 'Kathleen Mavourneen,' &c. The nigger melodies followed the Emancipation in 1833; then came Christy Minstrels, and after that the Deluge, Long to *rain* over us."

With regard to the songs of the end of the last and the beginning of this century, more shall be said in the notes on the songs that will be given in the collection.

There is one very important point that must be noticed here, as having had much to do with the history of English song. In no theatre except the two patent houses, Drury Lane and Covent Garden, was it lawful for actors to perform a drama. In others only burlettas and farces were legal. To evade the law, the performers were obliged to introduce songs, whether appropriate to the play or not. In some cases a piano was tinkled during the dialogue, so that the piece might escape condemnation in the Chancellor's Court, by being described as a musical performance. But this necessity to evade the law provoked musical invention, and brought into notice and popularity a number of songs that might otherwise have never been composed.

But we must retrace our steps somewhat, and with Tom d'Urfey consider the beginning of English song-books. Tom was a native of Exeter, of French extraction, who came to town, and became a favourite of Charles II. Not only did he produce operas into which he worked folk-songs, but he brought out "Pills to Purge Melancholy," a collection of songs, to a large extent original, mostly set to old English folk-airs. D'Urfey had a knack of writing with spirit, unhappily his was an uncleanly muse, and his six volumes (1719) are full of filth of the most disgusting character, of filth unredeemed by genuine humour. His dirt overflowed into subsequent collections, as "The Convivial Songster," 1782. The same publisher (J. Fielding), however, produced a companion volume, "The Vocal Enchantress," which is clear of this nastiness.

JOHN PLAYFORD.

To D'Urfey, or rather to John Playford, the music publisher, who worked with him, are due the preservation of a host of old English song tunes, which otherwise would have been entirely lost.

The following list of song-books with music that have been printed will be found useful. It is by no means exhaustive, and it does not include glee, madrigal, and catch books, but it does include some books of dance and virginal music where old song melodies are preserved:—

---

[1] Moore was by no means scrupulous whence he took the tunes for his "Irish melodies." A large percentage are demonstrably English, and some that were genuinely Irish he altered arbitrarily to please his taste, and give them a new sentimental character.

WHYTHORNE (T.), Songes of three, fower, and five voices, 1571.
BYRDE (WILLIAM), Songs of sundrie Nations, 1589.
DOWLAND (J.), Songs or Ayres of four Parts. First Book, 1595; second Book, 1600.
HOLBORNE (ANTHONY), Citharn Schoole, 1597.
MORLEY (T.), The first Book of Consort Lessons, 1599.
    ,,   ,,   of Ayres and Select Songs, 1600.
PILKINGTON (FR.). The first Book of Songs and Ayres, 1605.
ROBINSON'S School of Musicke, 1603.
    ,,   New Citharn Lessons, 1609.
FORD (T.), Musicke of Sundrie Kindes, 1607.
JONES (ROBT.), A Musical Dreame, 1609.
RAVENSCROFT (T.), Pammelia, 1609.
    ,,   Deuteromelia, 1609.
    ,,   Melismata, 1611.
WILSON (J.), Cheerful Ayres or ballads, 1609.
CORKINE (WM.), Ayres to sing and play to the lute and basse viol, 1st book 1610; 2nd book 1612.
COPRANO (JOHN), Songs of Mourning (on the death of Prince Henry). 1613.
WILSON (JOHN). Select Ayres and Dialogues, 1653.
LAWES (HENRY), Ayres and Dialogues, 1653–8.
    ,,   Court Ayres, 1655; reprinted 1662.
    ,,   The Treasury of Musick, 1669.
GAMBLE (JOHN), Ayres and Dialogues, 1656.
PLAYFORD (JOHN), An Antidote against Melancholy, 1661.
    ,,   The Musical Companion, 1667–73.
    ,,   Introduction to Musick, 1664.
Musick's Delight on the Cithren, 1666.
Musick's Recreation on the Lyra Viol, 1652.
Musick's Recreation on the Viol-Lyra-Way, 1661.
FORBES: Songs and Fancies, 1666.
Choice Songs and Ayres, 1673.
Choice Ayres, Songs, and Dialogues, 1676–84.
BOWMAN (HENRY), Songs for one, two, and three voyces, 1679.
The Musical Companion, 1667.
Comes Amoris, or the Companion of Love, *n.d.*, but. *circ.* 1680.
BANISTER (JOHN), and Low (THOMAS). New ayres and dialogues, 1678.
Apollo's Banquet, 1669, reprinted 1690, again 1693.
A choice Collection of 180 Loyal Songs, 1685.
D'URFEY (T.), Choice Songs, 1684.
The Theatre of Music, 1685–87; 1693–5.
The Banquet of Musick, a collection of the newest and best songs sung at Court, 1688–92.
GREETING (THOMAS), The Pleasant Companion, 1688.
Deliciæ Musicæ, a Collection of the newest and best songs, 1695–6.
[CARR (R.)], The Delightful Companion, 1686.
Musick's Handmaid, 1689.
Mercurius Musicus, 1699–1701.
KING (ROBERT). Songs for one, two, and three voices, *circ.* 1700.
ABELL (JOHN), A collection of songs in several languages, 1701.
ECCLES (JOHN), The songs and symphonies performed before her Majestie, 1703.
    ,,   General Collection of Songs, *circ.* 1704.
PURCELL (HENRY), Orpheus Brittanicus, 2 vols., all compositions of Purcell, 1697–1702.
    ,,   Songs in " Don Quixote," 1694.
    ,,   ,,   "The Indian Queen," 1695.
The Monthly Mask, 1704 (continued to about 1722).
RICHARDSON (V.), A collection of songs, 1706.
RAYMONDEN (L.), A New Book of Songs, *circ.* 1710.
The Merry Musician, in 3 vols., 1716, in 4 vols., 1730.
D'URFEY, Pills to purge Melancholy, 1st vol. 1700; in 2 vols., 1707; in 6 vols., 1719.
VANBRUGHE (GEORGE), Mirth and Harmony, *circ.* 1720.
The Pocket Companion, *circ.* 1725.
The Opera Miscellany, *circ.* 1725.

Leveridge (Richard). Collection of Songs, 1727.
The Musical Miscellany, in 6 vols., 1729-30.
The Excellent Choice, a collection of Popular airs, set by Dr. Pepusch, *circ.* 1728.
The British Musical Miscellany, in 6 vols., 1730.
The Vocal Miscellany, in 2 vols., 1734-8.
The Musical Entertainment, 1737.
British Melody, or, The Musical Magazine, *circ.* 1738.
Calliope, or English Harmony, in 2 vols., copperplate engravings above each song, 1739-50.
The Delightful Pocket Companion, *circ.* 1740.
The Musical Century, one hundred English Ballads, words and music by H. Carey, 2 vols., 1737-40.
Universal Harmony, with engraved head-pieces, 1745. This is a reproduction of an earlier work entitled "The English Orpheus." At the top of a few pages the older title is still legible, not having been properly erased.
Thesaurus Musicus, 2 vols, 1746. This is quite a distinct work from one of the same name published in 1693-6, in 5 books.
The Lyre, 1746.
Amaryllis, 1746; a second ed., in 2 vols., with engraved head-pieces, *circ.* 1756.
The Bulfinch, 1746.
Holcombe (H.). The Musical Medley, or a collection of English Songs, *n.d.*, but 1748.
An Antidote against Melancholy, 1749.
Social Harmony, 1750.
The Vocal Enchantress, 1750.
The Spinnet, 1750.
The Merry Companion, 1750.
Apollo's Cabinet, 2 vols., 1757.
Clio and Euterpe, in 3 vols., the first edition in 2 vols., 1758; that in 3, 1762. This, like Calliope, has engraved head-pieces.

After this date the number of published song-books with music becomes very great. Such then is an approximate list of the books of English songs that have issued from the press up to 1757. To these must be added the Ballad operas, of which a list has been given before, and the collections of Country Dances, of which a good list will be found in Mr. Kidson's "Country Dances," 1891. There are other sources, such as collections of Psalm and Hymn tunes. The Puritans would not let the devil have the best airs, and so appropriated them to sacred words. It was so with the Calvinists in Holland, and the Huguenots in France.

In the British Museum is a copy of "Psalmes or songs of Sion, turned into the language, and set to the tunes of a strange land, by W(illiam) S(latyer)," 1642. But, indeed, before that, a Dutch psalter printed at Antwerp, by Symon Lock, in 1540, contains little else but ballad and dance tunes; "Accursed be that False Old Man," "Upon the Bridge at Avignon," "Venus, Juno, Pallas," "The Nightingale, she sings a Song," "Le Berger et la Bergère sont à l'ombre d'un Buisson," were some of these. Few combinations could be more irreverent than the words of Psalm xxv., *Dominus illuminatio mea*," with the tune of "I knew a damsel amorous." The French psalters by Marot and Beza sinned quite as deeply in this respect; Psalm xxxviii. was sung to a jig, and Psalm xxxv. to a dance of Poitou.

Probably much the same thing exists in conventicles to the present day. An old singer said once to me, "If I go to chapel, I hear funny songs there. The words be gude enough, but the tunes—hang me, when I hears them, I wants to put the old words to 'em. But they always ties up the tails of these tunes in a fashion I don't like." What he meant was that the profane air was given a conventional hymn-like end that made it fit to be sung in public worship.

The collection of songs now presented to the public must not be taken to be more than a sample of what English Minstrelsy has been from the Tudor age to the end of the first half of the present century. It differs somewhat from other collections, having an independent aim in this, that it does not confine itself exclusively to published songs, by well-known composers.

The highest honour is due to the late Mr. William Chappell for his labours in the field of old English Music, of which "The Popular Music of Olden Time," 1855, is a *monumentum acre perennius*. But this work took little account of the living traditional song of the people, and the Editor of the new edition (1894) has excluded from the work all the traditional airs not found in print. Consequently this work is a monument erected over the corpses of dead melodies, which indeed it enshrines and preserves. It in no way represents the living music of the English people.

Mr. Hatton, in his "Songs of England," derives exclusively from printed sources, and only 46 of the 200 melodies are not by well-known composers.

As a National Monument of English Song, it seems only just that the music of all classes should be included in this work, that it should not confine itself to such songs as have been written for the harpsichord and the piano, by skilled musicians, but should include also the lark and thrush and blackbird song of the ploughman, the thrasher, and the milkmaid; that it should give songs as dear to their hearts as are "Cherry Ripe," "The Wolf," and "Love's Ritornella" to the gentlemen and ladies in the drawing-room.

The special charm of Scottish Minstrelsy consists in its being so entirely natural. The great bulk of English printed Minstrelsy was composed by accomplished musicians to words often having no relation to real life, and describe the amours of Corydons and Pastorellas in an ideal and fantastical world such as never existed.

The charm of the old and beautiful music has in many cases saved from death songs that express unreal sentiment, and they are loved and admired much as we love and admire old Chelsea china shepherds and shepherdesses; and as being really quaint and artistic, they deserve preservation, they are a part of our heritage, and they tell of a past stage of fashion that was as picturesquely absurd as that of the wig and the patch.

But let also the English folk-music be taken up into association with this, and the simplicity, the genuineness of the one gives an agreeable contrast to the affectation of the other. The English labourer is now an important factor in politics; that he has been a factor in English music has not been recognised as it ought. Of the freshness and sweetness of our English folk-airs one cannot speak too highly, and the time has now come when the music of the ploughboy demands to be recognised as an integral portion of our "English Minstrelsy," just as his opinion demands a hearing in all that concerns our commonwealth. Of English folk-song I shall treat in my Fourth Essay.

To my mind, the genuine English music of the last three hundred years has a charm possessed by none other. It appeals to my heart as does nothing French, German, and Italian. I do not suppose that I am a phenomenon on that account, but I believe that I have the audacity to say what thousands feel, but are afraid to admit.

One evening Mme. Malibran was in society where the conversation turned on the respective merits of the music of all nations. No one present would say a good word for that which was English. Some loudly declared that there was not one sound melody that was entirely and originally of English creation. Malibran rose in the midst of the discussion and offered to sing a new Spanish ballad, just introduced by Don Chocarreria. She commenced—the greatest attention prevailed; she touched the notes lightly, introduced variations, and sang, *adagio*—

> "Maria trayga un caldero
> De aqua, Llama levante
> Maria pon tu caldero
> Ayamos nuestro te."

She finished amidst immense applause, and an outcry that here was a case in point – a graceful, original air beyond the possibility of English musical conception. Malibran smiled, played the air again *presto*, to the original English words "Polly put the kettle on." Then—"Gentlemen," she said, "you have, even in your nurseries, charming airs, but because they are your own, you despise them."

On the healthy, unsophisticated nature, an English air has precisely the charm it ought. It has sprung out of the English heart, and it appeals to the English heart, only we are taught by a detestable fashion to steel ourselves against what is native in music. Let me tell one more anecdote, and I will hasten to a conclusion.

When Captain Montague was cruising off Brighton, Madame Catalani was invited to a brilliant *fête* on board his frigate. The captain went in his launch on shore, manned by over twenty men, to escort her on board. As the boat was cutting through the waves, Catalani unasked, and unexpectedly, burst forth in the song, "Rule Britannia." Had a voice from the deep spoken, the effect could not have been more instantaneous and thrilling.

The sailors' eyes kindled, their pulses leaped, the flush came into their cheeks, and as her glorious voice rang out the well-known loved strain, some of the men burst into tears.

"Madame," said Captain Montague, "the effect that this grand old English air has on these brave men, when sung by the finest voice in the world, is greater than the excitement I have seen in many a victorious battle I have been in."

AN HISTORICAL SKETCH OF ENGLISH NATIONAL SONG

There is a merit, doubtless, in being so wide hearted as to love all that is good and beautiful wheresoever it may be found, but surely it is narrowness of the most perverted description to be catholic to all but what is national, and one's own. What Henry Lawes said in 1653 is true still, and for the same reason precisely: "Whatsoever is native, be it ever so excellent, must lose its taste—to Englishmen, *because they have lost theirs*."

S. B. G.

LEW TRENCHARD, NORTH DEVON,
February 1895.

⁎⁎⁎ The initials, H. F. S., F. W. B., *and* W. H. H., *placed in brackets at the head of each song refer to the name of the arranger*—H. FLEETWOOD SHEPPARD, F. W. BUSSELL, *and* W. H. HOPKINSON, *respectively ; for the selection of songs the Editor is responsible.*

WAITS. *From a Broadside.*

NOTES TO SONGS

VOL. I.

God Save Our Gracious Queen (p. 2).—The National Anthem dates from about 1742, when it appeared in a collection of part songs, entitled, "Harmonia Anglicana," to which Purcell, Blow, Handel, Green, and other famous musicians of the time, contributed. The book was published by John Simpson, near the Royal Exchange.

Before the discovery of this version, which was made by Mr. William Chappell, the earliest known was that printed in *The Gentleman's Magazine*, for October 1745, which consists of the three stanzas which are still usually sung, and commences, "God save great George our King." At the same date, 1745, it was published on half-sheet broadside, as, "A Loyal Song. Sung at both Theatres. For Two Voices." Of this a copy is on the next page. The date of this sheet is fixed by verse 4, that runs thus—

> "O grant that Marshal Wade,
> May by Thy mighty Aid
>   Victory bring.
> May he sedition hush,
> And like a Torrent Rush
> Rebellious Scots to crush,
>   God save the King."

The verse relative to Wade fixes the date to a nicety. Prince Charles Edward had begun his march into England on October 31, 1745. Carlisle was entered on the 17th November. On the 20th the insurgents proceeded in two separate bands, which united at Preston. Marshal Wade was marching against him through Yorkshire. The Duke of Cumberland lay at Lichfield. The Chevalier, however, advanced as far as Derby, which he entered on December 5th, and London was in a panic. Almost certainly the version of "God save King George," which was sung in the London theatres as a duet, took this form in October, 1745. The hymn acquired immense popularity, evoked great enthusiasm, and became a great song of the Whigs.

The tune, as has been pointed out by Mr. Chappell, consists of two strains, of which the first has six measures, in groups of two, and the second eight, also in groups of two; and as this is a form of tune special to the galliard, a lively dance in triple time, it almost certainly leads to the conclusion that the hymn was composed to an already familiar galliard.

Now there was such a galliard, a composition of Dr. John Bull, transcribed in 1622, but not in the modern key of A major. The MS. containing this galliard belonged to Dr. Pepusch, and it is not improbable that Henry Carey, a contributor to the "Harmonia Anglicana," may have borrowed the book, and have altered the tune of Dr. Bull into the modern form it now wears. Carey never, himself, laid claim to have been the author of the National Anthem, but that claim was made for him by his son. Dr. Harrington, in a letter to the younger Carey, said, "Mr. Smith has often told me that your father came to him with the words and music, desiring him to correct the bass, which was not proper; and, at your father's request, Mr. Smith wrote another bass in correct harmony." This Mr. Smith was John Christopher Smith, the amanuensis of Handel.

Richard Clark, deputy-organist at Westminster Abbey, and then at the Chapels Royal, published in 1814 a volume of glees, madrigals, and catches, with a preface, in which is given an account of the National Anthem, and an attempt was made by him to prove that it was a composition by Carey. As his statements were contradicted, Clark set himself to find out fresh evidence, and after eight years research he proved, by a strong chain of circumstantial evidence, that the National Anthem was written by Ben Jonson, the music by Dr. Bull, and that it was first sung at Merchant Tailors' Hall, on July 7, 1607, by the gentlemen and children of His Majesty's Chapel Royal, when King James I. was present at a dinner given by that Company on his escape from the Gunpowder Plot. The words, "Frustrate their knavish tricks," applied very appropriately to the vile Popish intrigue. This curious account was published in 1821. After this work was before the public, Clark produced three tunes from MS. collections, and showed how that the identical melody of "God save the King" existed in the reign of Charles I., and was composed by Bull.

Unhappily, Clark did not treat his authorities quite legitimately. He added sharps to notes in the MSS. of Bull's music, so as to make the resemblance close where it did not exist as the air stood. Mr. Chappell says, "When Clark played the 'ayre' to me, with the book before him, I thought it to be the original of the National Anthem; but, afterwards, taking the MS. into my own hands, I was convinced that it had been tampered with, and the resemblance strengthened, the sharps being in ink of a much darker colour than other parts. The additions are very perceptible, in spite of Clark's having covered the face of that portion with varnish. In its original state the 'ayre' commenced with these notes—

The g being natural, the resemblance to 'God save the King' does not strike the ear, but by making the g sharp, and changing the whole from an old scale, without sharps or flats, into the modern scale A major (three sharps), the tune becomes *essentially* like 'God save the King.'"* At the same time, it is possible that all that Clark did was to ink over some of the incidentals which were in faded ink, for it is obvious that *some* must have occurred in the original galliard. For the whole story and sifting of the evidence I must refer to Mr. Wooldridge's new edition of Chappell's immortal work.

My own view of the case is that Bull's galliard is really the foundation of the National Anthem, and that the air got modified into the modern scale in the mouths of the people, who were getting unused to the old modes, and had a fancy for the new system. Then Carey shaped it, with the assistance of Smith, into the form by which it has been since generally known. See what is said on "Pastime with Good Company." The tune has also been attributed to Lully (*d.* 1687), and it has been pretended, nay asserted, that Handel brought it to England from France. It has been adapted to various German and other songs, as "Schalle der Freiheits-Sange," which was written by Follen, and published at Jena in 1819. But the very first words adapted to this air in any foreign language were written by a Dane in 1790, and the Prussian hymn, "Heil dir im Sieger Kranz," is much later than this (see extract from *Berliner Musik-Zeitung*, in *The Musical World* for February 29, 1868).

A curious story is told in the Memoirs of Raymond, the Drury Lane prompter, connected with "God save the King."

---

* The original MS. has disappeared, and cannot be traced.

At Weymouth, King George III. was caught by the rain whilst passing the theatre, and for shelter he entered, went into the Royal box, and seating himself in his own chair, fell into a comfortable doze. Elliston, the actor, who was also manager, went into the

2
O Lord our God arise,
Scatter his Enemies,
And make them fall:
Confound their Politicks,
Frustrate their Knavish Tricks,
On him our Hopes we fix,
God save us all.

3
Thy Choicest gifts in Store
On GEORGE be pleas'd to pour
Long may he reign
May he defend our Laws
And ever give us Cause
With Heart and Voice to Sing
God save the King.

4
O grant that Marshal WADE
May by thy mighty Aid
Victory bring
May he Sedition hush
And like a Torrent Rush
Rebellious Scots to crush
God save the King.

theatre, and seeing a man asleep in the Royal box, entered it with the intention of kicking him out. However, he recognised the king. The theatre had to be got ready for an approaching representation. What was to be done? Elliston hit on the following expedient: taking up a violin from the orchestra, he stepped into the pit, and placing himself just beneath his exalted guest, struck up the National Anthem. The royal sleeper unclosed his eyes, started up, and staring at the comedian exclaimed, "Hey! hey! what, what? Oh, I see, Elliston—ha, ha!—rain came on, took a nap. What's o'clock?" "Six o'clock, your Majesty." "Six o'clock! oh—ah! send to Her Majesty—tell her to bring my best wig. Don't keep the people waiting. Light up; I'll stay."

When Catalani had to sing "God save the King," being ignorant of English she had to acquire the words phonetically. Here is the copy of a verse on a card from which she learned the Anthem :—

> Oh Lord avar God,
> Arais schaetar
> Is enemis, and
> Mece them fol.
> Confond tear
> Politekse, frosstre
> Their nevise trix,
> On George avar hopes
> We fix. God save the Kin.

Pastime With Good Company (p. 4).—This song is given as a curiosity. It was composed by Henry VIII., both words and music, and is found in a MS. that contains several other compositions of the monarch, now in the British Museum.

In Wedderburn's "Complaynt of Scotland," 1549, there is mention of this song. "Now I will rehearse some of the sweet songs that I heard among them (the shepherds) as after follows, in the first *Pastance with Good Company*."

Pasqualigo, Venetian ambassador at the English Court, wrote of Henry: "He speaks French, English, and Latin, and a little Italian, plays well on the lute and virginals, sings from book at sight, draws the bow with greater strength than any man in England, and jousts marvellously." The titles of some of Henry's other songs are :—"Adeu, madam et ma mastres," "Alas what shall I do for love?" "O my hart and O my hart!" "Alac, alac, what shall I do?" "Grene groweth the holy." "It is to me a ryght gret joy."

In the original MS. the accidentals do not occur, but must be added, and were expected to be used.

Mr. Hullah, in one of his lectures on "The Third or Transition Period of Musical History," says, "Little reliance is to be placed on the accidentals found in early manuscript music, often inserted, as they evidently are, by a later hand. In some cases, no doubt, such insertion is the verification of a tradition, but in others it is simply the record of individual fancy." This applies to the copy of Bull's galliard that Clark produced as the original of "God save the King." He may not have added the sharps. Bull may have omitted to write them in, trusting to musicians understanding what was required. In "Pastime with Good Company," and the rest of the early music of the period of Henry VIII., they are omitted, and this is puzzling to those inexperienced in the reading of early musical notation.

There were certain rules of *Musica ficta*, which was a term used to express certain notes which, it was assumed, were chromatically raised or lowered a semitone in actual performance, but of which alteration no indication was given in the written parts. "These alterations," says the Editor to "Songs and Madrigals of the 15th Century," "said to have been made by singers and intended and sanctioned (though not indicated) by composers, may have come into use for the two reasons of harmonic propriety and of melodious smoothness.

"Without these additional but unwritten inflections, (1) certain dissonant harmonic combinations (or *chords*, as we should now call them) would have been called into existence, which the system of tuning then in vogue would have rendered more or less offensive to the ear; and (2) many passages of melody would have presented here and there rough edges and sharp corners, ungrateful alike to both singer and listener. It is, of course, very doubtful whether these accidentals were required or not; many musicians of the present day, who are skilled in reading old music, think that there was no fixed practice for their use. Our ears have grown so accustomed to modern tonalities, that it is exceedingly difficult for us to realise the old tonal feeling which possessed those who sang and wrote four centuries ago."* Another feature of the compositions of this period is that the air is to be looked for in the tenor. The faux Bourdons, so generally used in French churches, perpetuate the usage of the 16th century. There is an extremely curious and interesting book of songs belonging to the 15th and 16th centuries, that has been recently found in the library of the Escurial, written for the Duke of Alva; all are in four parts, and in nearly all, if not every one, the melody is in the tenor. "Pastime with Good Company" has been very happily arranged for the madrigal volumes recently issued by the "Early English Music Society." It has also been set by Mr. Wooldridge for the new edition of Chappell's work.

When once I Was a Shepherd Boy (p. 6).—This is a favourite folk-song throughout England. It is sung in Yorkshire and in Cornwall. Mr. Kidson, in his "Traditional Tunes," 1891, gives two airs to which he has heard it in the North of England, one of which is almost identical with that which is used in the West of England. The song is sometimes called "Little Fan;" at others, "Down in our Village." Its popularity is well attested by the way in which the words have been issued by nearly all the broadside publishers of the first half of the present century. I sent it to Messrs. Parlane, of Paisley, and they have issued it as a four-part song in their "National Choir." That this is a published song, probably a Vauxhall one, I have little doubt; but as yet I have not been able to find it.

Charming Phillis (p. 8).—This graceful little song is found in engraved copperplate, circ. 1732; also the air, without words, in Thompson's "Tutor for the Viol," circ. 1786; and in "The Compleat Tutor for the Hautboy," about 1750. In my childhood I remember this air very well, with the first verse as having been sung to me either by an aunt or by my nurse. The air was well engrained in my memory before I chanced on it in print. The title of the song in copperplate is "The Passionate Lover," and it runs in seven stanzas of four lines. The second portion seems to have been added later. The additional verse in the copperplate is—

> "Send an arrow, pierce her through;
> Oh, kind Cupid, see my grief;
> Make her kinder, let me find her
> Warm'd with love to give relief."

As Dolly sat Missing her Cow (p. 11).—A folk-song of the period of the middle or end of last century, but is almost certainly originally a Vauxhall or Ranelagh song. The words occur in "The Tomtit," Aldermary Churchyard, circ. 1780. In broadside the song appears under the title of "Bonny Hodge."

It was taken down from the singing of a farmer's two daughters, sisters, who sang it as a duet, as such it has accordingly been arranged.

The Vicar of Bray (p. 14).—Simon Aleyn, Canon of Windsor, was Vicar of Bray, in Berkshire, from 1540 to 1588. "He was a Papist under the reign of Henry VIII., and a Protestant under Edward VI.; he was a Papist again under Mary, and once more became a Protestant in the reign of Elizabeth. When

---

* "Songs and Madrigals of the 15th Century." Printed for the Plain Song and Mediaval Music Society, 1891.

this scandal to the gown was reproached for his versatility of religious creeds, and taxed for being a turncoat and an inconstant changeling," as Fuller says, "he replied, 'Not so neither; for if I changed my religion, I am sure I kept true to my principle; which is, to live and die the Vicar of Bray."

In a sermon preached before the Lord Mayor and Aldermen of London, in 1682, by John Evans, occurs an allusion to this notorious man. After describing a Moderate man as being, in fact, a man without definite convictions, the preacher says, "And if this be Moderation, the old Vicar of Bray was the most Moderate man that ever breathed."

Nichols, in his "Select Poems," says that the song of the Vicar of Bray "was written by a soldier in Colonel Fuller's troop of dragoons, in the reign of George I."

The air is far older than the words, and belonged originally to another song, "The Country Garden." This tune occurs in several Ballad Operas. The new song of "The Vicar of Bray" so completely displaced the old one of "The Country Garden," that the words of the latter have been completely lost.

In some copies, the tune is printed in ¾ time, which entirely alters its character, and makes of it a plaintive and gracefully flowing melody, and this, I venture to believe, was its original form.

Come Lasses and Lads (p. 18).—This delicious old song is one of the few in D'Urfey's "Pills to Purge Melancholy," which is not defiled by some coarseness.

The earliest copy known is found in the *Westminster Drollery*, part ii., 1672, and is entitled "The Rural Dance about the May-Pole: the Tune, the first Figure-Dance at Mr. Young's Ball, in May '71." In "Pills to Purge Melancholy," 1719, vol. iii., it is given with the music; but the air has been considerably altered in course of time.

Come if you Dare (p. 20).—A song in H. Purcell's *Masque of King Arthur*, the words of which were by Dryden. It appeared in 1691. The play was a sequel to the *Albion and Albanius* of the same author, and was written for the sake of the music and machinery, but has some dramatic merit. Henry Purcell was born in 1658, and died 1695, at the early age of thirty-seven. Many of Purcell's detached songs were published after his death in "Orpheus Britannicus: a Collection of Ayres, composed for the Theatre, and on other Occasions, by the late Mr. Henry Purcell. London, printed for Frances Purcell, executrix of the Author, 1697." The second edition appeared in 1706, and contains 33 airs not in the first edition. "Come if you dare" is not included in this collection.

Garrick revived *King Arthur* in 1770, and it was performed with some success at Drury Lane, when some additional songs were introduced.

Amo, Amas (p. 24).—This song was written by John O'Keefe, born 1746 in Dublin, for the Musical Farce, "The Agreeable Surprise," which was performed at the Haymarket in 1781. The music was arranged by Dr. Arnold. "The Agreeable Surprise" is formed on the pattern of the Ballad Operas that preceded it, the airs taken from every quarter, and "Amo, Amas" is headed, "The Frog and the Mouse." It is, in fact, an adaptation of this very ancient melody. "The Frog and the Mouse" was one of those songs which Wedderburn, in his "Complaint of Scotland," 1549, says was sung by shepherds in his time. It appears as a dance tune in "Walsh's Dances," for 1713; and, as the familiar Nursery Song, "The Carrion Crow," is still in use. The tune of "Little Bingo" is a modification of the same. Indeed it is curious to observe how this standard old English melody has formed the ground for a vast number of variations and adaptations. In its first form we have it in "Melismata," 1611.

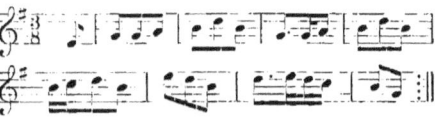

Then as a Country Dance— *From "Thompson's Pocket Companion for the German Flute, 1797."*

The very fine melody used by D'Urfey for his song, "Lord Frog and Lady Mouse," in "Pills to Purge Melancholy," 1719, vol. i., is quite distinct. This occurs in the Ballad Opera of "Achilles," 1733, to which is set the song, "Oh, then it seems you want a Wife."

O'Keefe's "Amo, Amas" has been a favourite with all schoolboys.

"Amo, Amas" got into "The Vocal Enchanter," 1782, and other song books, soon after the appearance of "The Agreeable Surprise."

Giles Scroggins (p. 26).—This humorous song was composed by William Reeve, organist of Totnes in 1781, and of St. Martin, Ludgate, in 1792. He was the author of a good many comic songs, and of pantomimes. "Giles Scroggins" has maintained its popularity to this day.

The air was not by Reeve, but was an old dance tune, accommodated by Reeve to the words he wrote. The same air, in Somersetshire form, will be found as "The Barley Straw" in our "Songs of the West." Reeve published his version in 1830. In the same year Rich employed the same air for Hunneman's "Old King Cole." The melody is quite out of character with the period and the other compositions of Reeve, and belongs to the 17th or early part of the 18th century.

Here's to the Maiden of Blushing Fifteen (p. 28). —The song was written by R. Brinsley Sheridan, and adapted by him or Linley to an old English melody, for his play of "The

School for Scandal," 1777. The second part of the air is the Country Dance, "Half Hannikin," given in the "Dancing Master" of 1650, and in subsequent editions. This was one of the dances performed at Whitehall at Christmas 1622. Sir H. Herbert, in his Office-book of Revels, says: "The Prince did lead the measures with the French Ambassador's wife," and "the masquers, with the ladies, did daunce two country dances, namely, *The Soldier's Marche*, and *Haff Hannikin.*"

The tune is not claimed by either Sheridan or Linley, and when published is usually signified to be "an old English air." It is so in "Lydian Leaves," vol. i., no date, but about 1820.

Taste a Bumper and Try (p. 30).—Often known by its initial line, "The women all tell me I'm false to my lass." It appears on copperplate engraved half-sheets between 1740 and 1750. The words are to be found in "The Bulfinch," 1746; "The Wreath," second ed., 1753; also in "The Convivial Songster," 1782. It does not occur in "The Musical Miscellany," 1729-30, nor in "The Hive," 1724-32, which it would inevitably have done had the song been then in existence. Its date may, therefore, be fixed at about 1740. John Parry took the song in hand, and added the roystering chorus that now gives the song its title; this was about 1835. It was again recast by Thomas Mitchell in 1850, and cut down to five verses. In the original it consists of double that number.

Where the Bee Sucks (p. 33).—The song of Ariel in *The Tempest*, wedded by Dr. Arne to equally immortal music. Thomas Augustine Arne was the son of an upholsterer in King Street, Covent Garden. His first serious attempt was in setting the music to Addison's *Rosamund*, in 1702. Then he wrote the music to Fielding's *Tom Thumb*, 1731. In 1738 his reputation as a lyric composer was established by his admirable setting of Milton's *Comus*. The melody of Arne at this time, and of his Vauxhall songs afterwards, forms an era in English music. He died in 1778. England must ever regard him as one of her most original and delightful musical composers.

Cherry Ripe (p. 36).—The words by R. Herrick, and the delightful air by C. E. Horn. Robert Herrick was vicar of Dean Prior in Devon. There he was buried in the churchyard in 1674. He was expelled from his living during the Protectorate; but lived to be reinstated under the Act of Uniformity. His poems contain many hits at his parishioners, whose manners, he says, "were rockie as their ways;" but they are full of the wild flowers —the daffodils and primroses—which abound in the orchards and steep hedgerows of Dean. Charles Edward Horn, the composer, was born in 1786, and was the son of Carl Frederick Horn, a German musician, who settled in London in 1782. Charles Edward produced a number of operas, none of which have lived. "Cherry Ripe" first appeared, set by Horn, in 1825.

I Went to the Fair (p. 40).—One of the songs that was sung by Madam Vestris. It was composed by John Whittaker.

Marigold Lane (p. 42).—A folk-air unhappily associated with objectionable words. It is one of two or three melodies employed to the same disagreeable ballad. I have therefore rewritten the song, as the tune has a certain pleasantness and pathos in it that deserve association with something better.

It is somewhat remarkable that so little attempt has been made in England to rescue fine old melodies from being lost through objectionable association. Any one who knows the originals of some of Allan Ramsay's, Burns's, Allan Cunningham's songs, set to traditional melodies, will see that they achieved a noble work in redeeming these excellent tunes from unworthy associations. I do not claim much merit for the air here given, but it is perhaps worthy of my words—which is not saying much. Anyhow it ought not to be allowed to be wholly lost.

Listen to the Voice of Love (p. 44).—The music to this favourite song is the composition of James Hook, born at Norwich in 1746. Hook was engaged as organist, first at Mary-le-bone Gardens, and then at Vauxhall, and this latter situation he held for from forty to fifty years. He composed a number of operatic pieces, none of which have lived. He was father of the Rev. Dr. Hook, prebendary of Winchester, and grandfather of Dr. Hook, the Vicar of Leeds and Dean of Chichester.

Down among the Dead Men (p. 46).—This very popular song is found first on half-sheet copperplate, as "A Health to the Memory of Queen Anne," to the tune of *Down among the Dead Men*. Swift quotes this song *à propos* of the defunct Whig "Examiner" (1710). See Johnson's Lives "Addison" (S. Johnson's Works, edit. 1792; vol. x., p. 96).

The tune is found in the third volume of "The Dancing Master," published by Pearson and Young 1728, and in Walsh's "Dancing Master," the third vol., circ. 1730.

A Damsel possessed of Great Beauty (p. 48).— The air to this song is known to the peasantry of all England. In the original it accompanies words of which the first verse runs as follows:—

"A damsel possessed of great beauty,
She stood at her own father's gate;
The gallant huzzars were on duty,
To view them this maiden did wait.
Their horses were cap'ring and prancing,
Their accoutrements shone as a star;
From the plains they were nearer advancing,
She espied her own gallant huzzar."

This is, however, too long and uninteresting a ballad to be here given. It has been printed from a stall copy by Dr. W. A. Barrett, in his "English Folk Songs," No. 13. It is issued in broadside by Fortey, Such, &c., and is generally entitled, "Young Edward, the Gallant Hussar." The air, which has a striking character, has been adapted to a goodly number of modern comic songs. Fresh words have been written to this air, retaining of the original only the initial line.

The Bailiff's Daughter of Islington (p. 50).—This ancient ballad is found in the Roxburgh, Pepys, and Douce Collections. It was formerly sung to the tune of "I have a Good Mother at Home." It is given as "The Bailey's Daughter of Islington" in the ballad-opera of "The Jovial Crew," 1731. We give only a portion of the original ballad. The air seems to have originally belonged to another ballad, entitled "The Jolly Pindar."

From "The Jovial Crew."

This is a noble melody, and whether the traditional tune be a corruption of this, or a distinct air, and if so, what is its origin, is difficult to say.

The Friar of Orders Grey (p. 52).—The words of this song, that has maintained its hold on the popular taste, were

NOTES TO SONGS

by John O'Keefe, and the music by William Reeve, of whom a short notice has already been given.

Sweet Nelly, my Heart's Delight (p. 56).—A song that was vastly popular at the beginning of the 18th century, and was entitled, "The Farmer's Son." It is found in "The Merry Musician; or, A Cure for the Spleen," 1716, and in Watt's *Musical Miscellany*, i. 130 (1729), and in Walsh's *British Musical Miscellany*, 1730. The air was introduced into several Ballad Operas, as "The Lover's Opera," and "The Footman." It occurs also in engraved half-sheet songs. In the "Pepys' Collection of Broadsides," v. 216, is one of Charles II.'s reign, "The Conquer'd Lady; or, The Country Wooing between Robin, the Rich Farmer's Son, and Madam Nelly, a Nobleman's Daughter, &c. Tune of *The Milking Pail*." It begins—

"Young Nelly, my heart's delight."

In the original there are six stanzas. The girl answers Robin in two and a half.

It may be observed that the melody at "For love I profess, I can do no less, you have my favour won," is identical with that in the second line of "Come, Lasses and Lads."

The Farmer's Boy (p. 58).—One of the most popular and widely-known folk-songs in England. It would be hard to find an old labourer who has not heard it. It is still printed by Messrs. Howard, Great Marlborough Street, and by Mr. W. Paxton, 19, Oxford Street, London. Mr. Kidson gives four versions as acquired in Yorkshire.

The words were printed by Bell in his "Songs of the English Peasantry." He says, "The date of the composition may probably be referred to the commencement of the last century." An interesting circumstance may be mentioned in connection with this song. Not then knowing the traditional air, Mr. Sheppard set it to one of his own, and very delightful it was. Some twelve years ago, I sang this at a village concert, when an old labourer stood up, and saying to those near him, "He's got the words right, but the tune be all wrong—I b'ain't going to listen to old songs spoiled wi' new-fangled moosic," he left the room. This was what first drew my attention to the fact that there was extant, among our peasantry, a body of folk-melody that had never been collected.

The Wolf (p. 61).—A composition by William Shield. The words by O'Keefe. Shield was a native of Newcastle-upon-Tyne. He became musical director of Covent Garden Theatre at the close of last century. He composed a number of operas, which are dead without hope of resurrection, but several of his songs, such as "The Thorn," "The Heaving of the Lead," and "Old Towler," have retained their hold on the popular fancy. "The Wolf" has succeeded mainly because it is an easy and effective exercise for a bass voice, rather than for any musical merit in itself. For the sake of its bravura it is especially dear to amateur bass singers. This song was introduced into the ballad-opera of "The Castle of Andalusia" (published in 1798).

The Northern Lass (p. 66).—There are several songs that go by this name; one that begins "There was a lass of Cumberland," which is coarse; another of one Betty Maddox of Doncaster; and a third the tune to which was composed by William Fisher of Hereford, and this appears in the first vol. of "Calliope, or British Harmony," 1739, p. 81. "The Northern Lass" was a comedy by Richard Brome, acted in 1632. It was revived in 1684; new songs were added to it by Daniel Purcell, brother of the more famous Henry Purcell, who contributed several airs to

D'Urfey's "Pills to Purge Melancholy," but, as has been remarked of his melodies, "These have in general but little to recommend them, and their author is at this day better known for his puns, with which the old jest-books abound, than for his musical compositions."

Daniel Purcell's music to "The Northern Lass" was published in 1706. We give the song and air by Fisher; which became very popular, and appears as a copperplate half-sheet, with head-piece, which is reproduced on p. xxxi., and in another earlier half-sheet ballad with music without engraved headpiece. The song was first printed in 1730, under the title "Come, come, take your glass."

I've Been Roaming (p. 68).—The words are variously attributed to George Soame, and to Darley, who was also on the staff of the *Athenæum*, in which the verses first appeared. The music is by C. E. Horn. Miss Paton, when in her prime, was wont to make one of her greatest effects in this ballad.

Lubin's Rural Cot (p. 73).—A song noted from the singing of an old mason in Devonshire. I took down only one verse and a part of the second from the old ballad-singer; he had forgotten the rest of the words, and I have therefore completed the song to the best of my ability. The original is probably to be found somewhere in the compositions of the first half of last century, but I have not been fortunate enough to light on it. The air is pleasing and characteristic of the period, and quite unlike the genuine folk airs of the English peasants. It is remarkable as an instance of the traditional precision of our peasant singers. The old horrible twirls and flourishes that disfigure an otherwise good melody, have been retained and handed down exactly for a century and a half. Mr. Bussell has been reluctant to exscind them.

Galloping Dreary-dun (p. 76).—A song from "The Castle of Andalusia," a comic opera arranged by Dr. Arnold. The words by O'Keefe. It was acted at Covent Garden in 1782, and was an alteration from "The Banditti," an earlier play by the same author, that had not been successful. Mrs. Inchbald says of O'Keefe, "A reader must be acquainted with O'Keefe on the stage, to admire him in the closet. Yet he is entitled to more praise, in being the original author of a certain species of drama, made up of whim and frolic, than numberless retailers of wit and sentiment, with whom that class of readers are charmed, who are not in the habit of detecting plagiarism." The structure of this sentence is awkward, and the meaning not very clear. What Mrs. Inchbald probably meant was that O'Keefe introduced the comic opera of a new type to that of the "Beggar's Opera" and its imitations. And this is true; O'Keefe did this, and he gave us comic operas without grossness, and with good fun. The arrangement of "The Castle of Andalusia," by Dr. Arnold, followed the tradition of "The Beggar's Opera," the airs were nearly all borrowed. Some are by Handel, others by Vento, Giordani, Bertini, Giardini, Dr. Arne, and Carolan, the Irish bard. But "Galloping Dreary-dun," Dr. Arnold developed out of the same tune that Linley employed for "Here's to the Maiden." The accompaniment he provided is of the most meagre description.

The song got into *The Vocal Enchantress* the same year that the opera was performed, and before the music was published.

Should He Upbraid (p. 78).—This favourite piece is by Sir H. Bishop. The words by Shakespeare, and occurs in "The Two Gentlemen of Verona."

The Garden Gate (p. 84).—A song, the words of which were by W. Upton, and the music by W. T. Parke.

Bell included this song in his "Songs and Ballads of the English

2
If from the north such beauty comes
　How is it that I feel
Within my breast that glowing heat
　No tongue can e're reveal
Tho cold and raw the north wind blows
　All summer's on her breast
Her skin was like the driven snow
　But sun-shine all the rest

3
Her heart may southern climates melt
　Tho' frozen now it seems
That joy with pain be equal felt
　And ballanc'd in extreams.
Then like our genial wine she'll charm
　With love my panting breast
Me, like our sun her heart shall warm
　- Be Ice to all the rest.

Peasantry," not knowing its origin. He says of it: "One of the most pleasing ditties. The air is very beautiful. We first heard it sung in Malham dale, Yorkshire, by Willy Bolton, an old Dales' minstrel, who accompanied himself on the union-pipes."

The song was published in 1809. Mr. Bell heard it sung in Yorkshire, somewhere about 1856-60; so that the song took half a century to be, so to speak, naturalised among the Yorkshire peasantry. I have myself heard it sung by a little blacksmith who goes by the nickname of "Ginger Jack," and from whom I have taken down a great many songs, new and old. Mr. Sheppard also noted it down from a crippled stone-breaker, whose memory was richly furnished with old songs. Alas! the dear old man, for whom I had a particular regard, is dead. He was found stiff in a ditch one bitter winter night.

That the song became popular is shown by its having descended to the condition of broadside. As such it was issued by Catnach, Pitts, Fortey, Such, &c. Moreover, an "Answer to his Garden Gate," that is to say, a sequel, was published by the broadside ballad printers.

When that I Was a Little Tiny Boy (p. 86).—A song from *Twelfth Night*, where it is the Fool's song, sung on the stage as an epilogue. Its use there is due solely to theatrical tradition, and probably it was an old song in Shakespeare's time.

A song of the same description, and with the same burden, is sung by the Fool in *King Lear*, act iii. scene 2.

> "He that has and a little tiny wit,
> With heigh-ho! the wind and the rain,
> Must make content with his fortunes fit,
> For the rain it raineth every day."

The tune is traditional. Linley wrote a fresh air to the song, but this has not displaced the ancient melody.

The Flying Dutchman (p. 88).—A fine composition by the younger Parry, John Orlando, son of the "elder" Parry. The words are by R. Ryan, and the song was published in 1848.

Rocked in the Cradle of the Deep (p. 92).—The words of this fine song were by Mrs. Willard, and the music by Joseph Philip Knight. It was composed by him about 1840, while in America. He died 1st June 1887. Emma Willard (1787-1870), who wrote the words, was an American, the daughter of Samuel Hart, and married Dr. John Willard in 1809. She wrote for and promoted the higher education of women, and was head of the Troy seminary. Her schoolbooks were at one time much used.

I'm Afloat, I'm Afloat (p. 94).—One of the numerous catchey airs produced by Henry Russell, who was born in 1813. The words by Eliza Cook, born 1818; the song appeared in 1843, and found its way to every music hall, and then to the barrel organs, and was sung and ground to death. This has been the fate of Russell's airs—they have no great merit in them, but are catchey.

Simon the Cellarer (p. 97).—A song of Joseph L. Hatton, who did so much for old English songs, rescuing them from the rubbish to which they had been linked by J. Oxenford and Dr. Mackay, or restoring the old words to their proper place, and giving them tasteful and suitable accompaniments. The words of this song are by W. H. Bellamy. It was published in 1847.

We Met, 'Twas in a Crowd (p. 100).—Thomas H. Bayley has enriched English minstrelsy with several songs that have stood. Of these, "I'd be a Butterfly" is perhaps the best known. Bayley was born in 1797, and died 1831. The song, "We met, 'twas in a Crowd," appeared about 1828.

Poor Jack (p. 102).—Charles Dibdin was the most prolific of all song-writers. His compositions were very unequal. In the summer of 1788, having fallen out with the managers of the theatres in London, Dibdin resolved on going to India, where his brother had lately died, leaving, it was supposed, considerable property, especially a sum of £3500 due to him from the Nabob of Arcot. The vessel in which Dibdin sailed was driven by stress of weather into Torbay, where he abandoned his intention, and returned to London. Instead of applying to the theatres for an engagement, he determined, in his own words, "to put himself forward, and try his chance once more with the public." He wrote an entertainment entitled, "The Whim of the Moment," consisting of recitations and songs. Dibdin sat at a harpsichord and accompanied his own songs, but did not dress in character. "The Whim of the Moment" was produced in October 1788, and performed at intervals till the following April. Poor Dibdin was, however, arrested almost immediately for debt, and was lodged in King's Bench prison throughout this period, so that he could only give his entertainment during Term times, under permission from the Court. "The Whim of the Moment" was a failure in a pecuniary sense; nevertheless, Dibdin saw that his entertainment gave great pleasure to those who attended, and he was encouraged to pursue the same line. This he did, and for about twenty years, generally from October to April, he gave performances, and for these composed eighteen original entertainments.

"Poor Jack" was the most successful piece in "The Whim of the Moment."

The Months of Old (p. 106).—By Stephen Glover, in 1842, and is perhaps the best of the compositions of this popular composer, though not one that has most taken with the vulgar, probably for that very reason. The words were by William Jones.

The Spider and the Fly (p. 108).—A song by the popular song-writer Thomas Hudson, and was published by Williams of Paternoster Row, in 1853, with accompaniments and symphonies by W. Wilson; and again without name of composer in 1855. It was also arranged by E. J. Loder in 1861. The air is probably an old nursery jingling melody, as it was the way with Hudson to write his songs to familiar old airs. Glover's "Jeanette and Jeanot" is based on the same strain. This was a song much sung by Henry Russell.

In the Bay of Biscay (p. 111).—John Davy, the author of this imperishable song, was a native of Devonshire. Before he was six years old, a blacksmith, into whose house he was wont to run, missed between twenty and thirty horseshoes. Diligent search was made for them, but to no purpose. Not long afterwards the smith heard some musical sounds, which seemed to issue from the upper part of the house, and stealing upstairs, discovered little Davy in the attic. The boy had hung eight horse-shoes so as to form an octave, and was striking them with a small hammer, in imitation of Crediton chimes. When aged about twelve, he was articled to Jackson, the organist of Exeter Cathedral. He composed some dramatic pieces for the theatre at Sadler's Wells, and wrote the music to some operas that have not lived. He died in 1824. "In the Bay of Biscay" first appeared, in the ballad-opera of "Spanish Dollars," in 1805. The words by A. Cherry.

God save the Queen.

*For Solo or Quartett play the accompaniment *p* for Chorus play *f* with Bass in Octaves.

2
O Lord our God arise,
Scatter her enemies
    And make them fall.
Confound their politics:
Frustrate their knavish tricks:
On Thee our hopes we fix:
    God save the Queen.

3
Thy choicest gifts in store,
On her be pleased to pour,
    Long may she reign!
May she defend our laws,
And ever give us cause
To sing with heart and voice
    God save the Queen.

Pastime with Good Company.
King Henry VIII.

3
Company with honesty
Is virtue: and vice to flee.
Company is good or ill,
But every man hath his free-will.
　The best I sue,
　The worst eschew;
　　My mind shall be
Virtue to use,
Vice to refuse,
　I shall use me.

3
My dad and mam cry, "Fie! for shame!"
   Then laugh and joke and jeer me;
Think I'm too young, and much to blame
   And want from Fan to tear me;
But lads and lasses, dad and mam,
   And sowing, plough and tillage,
I'll give up all for little Fan,
   Down, down in our village.
       CHORUS. I'll give up all, &c.

4
But I don't mean to leave my home,
   For Fanny yet to marry;
Till money we've both saved a sum,
   We are resolved to tarry;
But then the village bells shall ring,
   No sowing, plough and tillage,
Then Fan shall dance, and I will sing,
   Down, down in our village.
       CHORUS. Then Fan shall dance, &c.

CHARMING PHYLLIS.

Old English Air. (H. F. S.)

Smoothly and with expression. ♩. = 112.

Key G.
Charm - ing Phyl - lis, fair as lil - ies,

But her will......... is to......... dis - dain.

2

Breath like roses June discloses,
  Sweet as posies, fragrant smell;
Brisk and airy like a fairy,
  Charms that Nature doth excel.
Ever pleasing, never teasing,
  Yet she's freezing, cold as snow,
To her lover, who to move her
  Melting language does bestow.

3

Lovely jewel, be not cruel,
  Quench my fuel, see me burn,
See me languish, ease my anguish,
  Turn, O! lovely charmer turn.
Grant your favour, and I ever
  Will endeavour to adore;
I'll caress thee, and will bless thee
  With true love for evermore.

As Dolly sat milking.
DUET.

3

The cow, who perceived in a trice
    That Dolly neglected her call,
And attended to Cupid's advice,
    Kicked over the milkpail and all,
"If these be your tricks," Hodge he cries
    "I'll away to my kindlier Betty."
"Let the cow go!" says Dolly, and then, with fond sighs,
    "Come back bonny Hodge, and I'll let ye!
        I will let ye! I will let ye!
    Come back bonny Hodge, and I'll let ye!"

4

Young Hodge he returnèd in haste,
    And kissed the fair maid with a smile.
She answered, "no time let us waste,
    But away to the church, o'er yon stile."
So the parson this couple did join;
    And now this young Dolly so pretty,
Says no more to young Hodge, with a flout and a frown
    When he asks for a kiss, "I'll not let ye!
        I'll not let ye! I'll not let ye!
    When he asks for a kiss, I'll not let ye!"

THE VICAR OF BRAY

COME, LASSES AND LADS.

1671 (W. H. H.)

3

Then after an hour they went to a bow'r,
  And play'd for ale and cakes,
And kisses too,—until they were due,
  The lasses held the stakes.
The girls did then begin
  To quarrel with the men,
And bade them take their kisses back,
  And give them their own again.

4

Now there they did stay, the whole of the day,
  And tired the fiddler quite
With dancing and play, without any pay,
  From morning until night.
They told the fiddler then
  They'd pay him for his play,
And each a twopence, twopence, twopence,
  Gave him, and went away.

5

Good-night, says Harry, good night, says Mary,
  Good-night, says Poll to John;
Good-night, says Sue to her sweetheart Hugh,
  Good-night, says ev'ry one.
Some did walk and some did run,
  Some loiter'd on the way,
And bound themselves by kisses twelve,
  To meet the next holiday.

Come, If You Dare.

H. PURCELL. (W. H. H.)

AMO AMAS.

Old English Air. (H. F. S.)

Repeat in Chorus.

2

Can I decline a nymph divine,
   Whose voice as a flute is dulcis,
Her oculos bright, her manus white
   And soft, when I tacts, her pulse is.
     CHORUS. Horum, Corum, etc.

3

O how bella my puella,
   I'll kiss saecula saeculorum,
If I have luck, Sir, she's my uxor,
   O dies benedictorum.
     CHORUS. Horum, Corum, etc.

Giles Scroggins.

3

Poor Mary laid her down to weep,
  Fol-lol-de-rol de-rol de-ra.
And cried herself quite fast asleep;
  Fol-de-rol-de fol-de-rol.
When, standing all by the bed post,
A figure tall her sight engross'd;
And cried, "I be poor Scroggin's ghost!"
  Fol-lol-de-rol-de rid-dle-de.

4

The ghost it said all solemnly
  Fol-lol-de-rol de-rol de-ra.
"O Molly, you must go with I!
  Fol-de-rol-de fol-de-rol.
Come, come before the morning beam."
"I won't," she cried, and gave a scream:
Then woke and found she'd dream'd a dream.
  All about, Fol-lol-de-rol-de rid-dle-de.
    (spoken)

HERE'S TO THE MAIDEN OF BASHFUL FIFTEEN.

Words by R. B. SHERIDAN.
Old English air adapted.
(W. H. H.)

3

Here's to the maid with a bosom of snow,
  Now to her that's as brown as a berry;
Here's to the wife with a face full of woe!
  And now to the damsel that's merry.
Let the toast pass, drink to the lass;
  I warrant she'll prove an excuse for the glass.
    CHORUS. Let the toast pass, etc.

4

Let her be clumsy or let her be slim,
  Young or ancient, I care not a feather;
Fill up your glasses — nay, fill to the brim,
  And let us e'en toast them together.
Let the toast pass, drink to the lass;
  I warrant she'll prove an excuse for the glass.
    CHORUS. Let the toast pass, etc.

Take a Bumper and try.

Old English Air. (H. F. S.)

2

Her lilies and roses were just in their prime,
Yet lilies and roses are conquer'd by time;
But in wine from its age such a benefit flows
That we like it the better, the older it grows.
Let murders, and battles, and history prove
The mischiefs that wait upon rivals in love;
In drinking, thank heaven, no rival contends,
For the more we love liquor, the more we are friends.
    O wine, mighty wine! etc.

3

She too might have poison'd the joy of my life,
With nurses, and babies, with squalling and strife,
But wine neither nurses nor babies can bring,
And a jolly big bottle's a mighty good thing.
Perhaps, like her sex, ever false to their word,
She'd left me, to get an estate, or a lord;
But my bumper, regardless of title and pelf,
By me will it stand, when I can't stand myself.
    O wine, mighty wine! etc.

WHERE THE BEE SUCKS.

(Ariel's song in "The Tempest.")

Dr ARNE. (W. H. H.)

Cherry ripe.

Words by R. HERRICK.
CHARLES E. HORN.
(W. H. H.)

I WENT TO THE FAIR.

Composed by J. WHITAKER.
(H. F. S.)

MARIGOLD LANE.

Folk Air. (F. W. B.)

2

I carried her satchel each morning to school,
O she was a scholar, but I was a fool;
    She help'd me to spell,
    And to cypher as well,
When I said, pri' thee Jane, out of Marigold Lane!
    O Jane, when again, etc.

3

When I had a slate and a copy to write,
If Jane were not by me, then sad was my plight,
    Writing J. N. E. Jane,
    Then those letters again,
And just nothing but _ Jane, out of Marigold Lane.
    O Jane, when again, etc.

4

So wretched a scholar, I ran off to sea,
And have not seen England for years ten and three
    But never my heart
    Lets the image depart,
Of that dear little Jane, out of Marigold Lane.
    O Jane, when again, etc.

5

But when I return to old England at last,
With gold in my pocket, my voyages past,
    Then I'll say, Pretty wench,
    Shall we sit on one bench?
And to lessons again _ now in Honeymoon Lane?
    O Jane, when again, etc.

LISTEN TO THE VOICE OF LOVE.

HOOK. (W. H. H.)

2
Where flowers their blooming sweets exhale,
  My Daphne let us fondly stray,
Where whisp'ring love breathes forth his tale,
  And shepherds sing their artless lay,
O listen, listen to the voice of love,
He calls my Daphne to the grove.

3
Come share with me the sweets of spring
  And leave the town's tumultuous noise;
The happy swains all cheerful sing,
  And echo still repeats their joys:
Then listen, listen to the voice of love,
He calls my Daphne to the grove.

DOWN AMONG THE DEAD MEN.

2

Let charming beauty's health go round,
In whom celestial joys are found:
And may confusion still pursue
The senseless woman-hating crew;
And they that women's health deny,
Down among the dead men let them lie.

3

May love and wine their rites maintain,
And their united pleasures reign!
While Bacchus' treasure crowns the board,
We'll sing the joys that both afford!
And they that won't with us comply,
Down among the dead men let them lie.

A Damsel Possessed of Great Beauty.

Folk air. (F. W. B.)

2
A damsel possessed of great beauty,
　And another possessed of great wealth;
I think I would quickly discover,
　The which I would put on the shelf.
For contentment, and comfort and pleasure,
　Are bred of a plentiful dower.
But beauty, and nothing but beauty,
　It fadeth from hour to hour.

3
A damsel possessed of great beauty,
　Without virtue and prudence combined,
Is about the most risky possession,
　And brittle, a mortal may find.
But with honour and virtue united
　On that man may safely rely.
For such has the choicest of beauties.
　With such I will live and will die.

E. I. d.

The Bailiff's Daughter of Islington.

17th Cent. (W. H. H.)

3

Before I give you a penny, sweetheart,
  Pray tell me where you were born;
At Islington, kind sir, she said,
  Where I have had many a scorn.
I prithee, sweetheart, tell to me,
  O tell me if you know
The bailiff's daughter of Islington?
  She is dead, sir, long ago.

4

If she is dead, then take my horse,
  My saddle and bridle also,
For I will to some far country,
  Where no man shall me know.
O stay, O stay, thou goodly youth
  She standeth by thy side!
She is here, alive, she is not dead,
  And ready to be thy bride.

I Am a Friar of Orders Grey.

Words by JOHN O'KEEFE.　　　　　　　　　　　　REEVE. (W. H. H.)

Sweet Nelly, my Heart's delight.

2
My father has riches in store,
Two hundred a year, and more;
   Besides sheep and cows,
   Carts, harrows and ploughs:
His age is above three score;
  And when he does die,
  Then, merrily I
Shall have what he has won;
   Both land and kine,
   All shall be thine,
   If thou'lt incline
   And wilt be mine,
And marry a farmer's son.

3
Dear Nelly, believe me, now,
I solemnly swear and vow,
   No lords in their lives
   Take pleasure in wives,
Like we that do drive the plough:
  Whatever we gain
  With labour and pain,
We don't into riot run,
   As courtiers do;
   And never I know
   A London beau
   That could outdo
A country farmer's son.

The Farmer's Boy.

Folk Song. (H. F. S.)

3

"And if that you no boy do want,
One favour I've to ask,
If you'll shelter me till break of day,
From this cold winter's blast;
At the break of day I will haste away,
Else-where to seek employ,
To plough and sow, and reap and mow,
 And be a farmer's boy."
CHORUS. To plough and sow, &c.

4

"Come try the lad," the mistress said,
Let him no longer seek;
"Yes, father, do," the daughter cried,
While the tears roll'd down her cheek:
"He'd work if he could, 'tis hard to want food,
And wander for employ,
Don't send him away, but let him stay,
 And be a farmer's boy."
CHORUS. To plough and sow, &c.

5

The farmer's boy grew up a man,
And the good old couple died,
They left the lad the farm they had,
And the daughter for his bride:
Now the lad which was and the farm now has,
Often smiles and thinks with joy,
Of that lucky day, when he came that way,
 To be a farmer's boy.
CHORUS. To plough and sow, &c.

Chorus.

THE WOLF.

The Northern Lass.

Old English Air. (H. F. S.)

2

If from the North such beauty came,
   How is it that I feel
Within my breast that glowing flame,
   No tongue can e'er reveal?
Though cold and raw the north-wind blow
   All summer's in her breast,
Her skin is like the driven snow,
   But sunshine all the rest.

3

Her heart may southern climates melt,
   Though frozen now it seems;
That joy with pain be equal felt,
   And balanced in extremes.
Then, like our genial wine, she'll charm
   With love my panting breast,
Me, like our sun, her heart shall warm,
   Be ice to all the rest.

I'VE BEEN ROAMING.
CAVATINA.

Words by GEORGE SOANE.   C. E. HORN. (W. H. H.)

LUBIN'S RURAL COT.

Folk song. (F. W. B.

GALLOPING DREARY DUN.

Composed by Dr ARNOLD.
(H. F. S.)

2
I saddled his steed so fine and so gay,
    Galloping dreary dun;
I mounted my mule, and we both rode away,
    With our haily, gaily, etc.

3
We canter'd along until it grew dark,
    Galloping dreary dun;
The nightingale sang instead of the lark,
    With her haily, gaily, etc.

4
We met with a friar, and ask'd him the way,
    Galloping dreary dun;
By my troth, says the friar, you've both gone astray,
    With your haily, gaily, etc.

5
Our journey, I fear, will do us no good,
    Galloping dreary dun;
We wander alone, like the babes in the wood,
    With our haily, gaily, etc.

6
I heard a shot fir'd, and I'll take a peep,
    Galloping dreary dun;
But now I think better, I'd better go sleep,
    With my haily, gaily, etc.

SHOULD HE UPBRAID.

Words by SHAKSPEARE.
Sir H. R. BISHOP.

THE GARDEN GATE.

Words by UPTON.
Music by W. T. PARKE. (W. H. H.)

2

She pac'd the garden here and there,
  The village clock struck nine;
When Lucy cried in wild despair,
  "He sha'n't, he sha'n't be mine!
Last night he vowed the garden gate
Should find him there this eve at eight;
But this I'll let the creature see,
He ne'er shall make a fool of me."

3

She ceas'd ‿ a voice her ear alarms,
  The village clock struck ten:
When William caught her in his arms,
  And ne'er to part again.
He shewed the ring, to wed next day,
He'd been to buy, a long, long way;
How then could Lucy cruel prove
To one that did so fondly love?

When that I was a little tiny Boy.

(From Shakespeare's "Twelfth Night.")

Old English Air.
(W. H. H.)

THE FLYING DUTCHMAN.

Words by RICHARD RYAN.
JOHN PARRY Junr.

3

He scuds along too rapidly to mark his eagle flight,
And lightning-like the Dutchman's helm is full soon out of sight.
p The crews of ships far distant now shudder at the breeze
cres. That bears dread Vanderdecken in fury o'er the seas.
p slower Then mourn the Flying Dutchman for terrible his doom,
f quicker The ocean round the stormy Cape, it is his living tomb!
There Vanderdecken beats about for ever, night and day,
And tries in vain to keep his vow by entering the bay.—

ROCKED IN THE CRADLE OF THE DEEP.

Words by Mrs. WILLARD. Music by J. P. KNIGHT.
(W. H. H.)

I'm Afloat.

Words by ELIZA COOK.
Con Spirito.

HENRY RUSSELL.
(W. H. H.)

Key F.

I'm a-float, I'm a-float on the star-light-ed sea, Give the "Sea-bird" her can-vas, and let her run free. I'm a-float, I'm a-float, I am king of my crew. Up, up with the red flag and

We have left the dull earth we're a-lone on the sea, Let the bum-pers go round, boys, and drink to the free. Let the bright wine be pour-ing as fast as the tide. Here's a health to the "Sea-bird" our

3

Old Simon reclines in his highback'd chair,
   And talks about taking a wife;
And Margery often is heard to declare
   She ought to be settled in life,
   She ought to be settled in life:
But Margery has (so the maids say) a tongue,
And she's not very handsome, and not very young:
So somehow it ends with a shake of the head,
And Simon he brews him a tankard instead.
While ho! ho! ho! He will chuckle and crow,
What! marry old Margery? no, no, no!
While ho! ho! ho! He will chuckle and crow.
What! marry old Margery? no, no, no!

WE MET.

Words and Music by T. H. BAYLEY.
(W. H. H.)

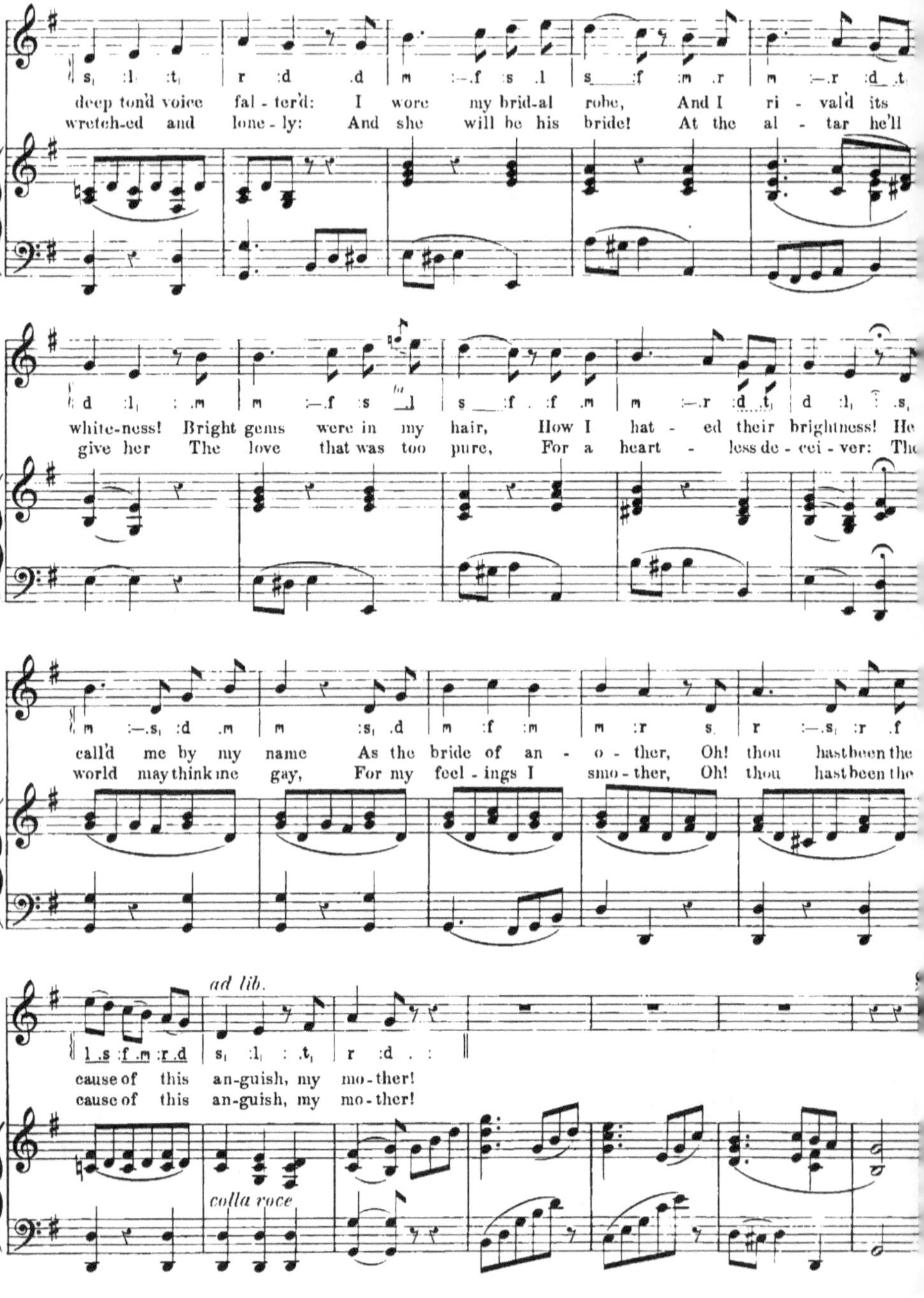
deep ton'd voice fal - ter'd: I wore my brid-al robe, And I ri - val'd its
wretch-ed and lone - ly: And she will be his bride! At the al - tar he'll
white-ness! Bright gems were in my hair, How I hat - ed their brightness! He
give her The love that was too pure, For a heart - less de - cei - ver: The
call'd me by my name As the bride of an - o - ther, Oh! thou hast been the
world may think me gay, For my feel - ings I smo - ther, Oh! thou hast been the
ad lib.
cause of this an-guish, my mo - ther!
cause of this an-guish, my mo - ther!
colla voce

Poor Jack.

C. DIBDIN (W. H. H.)

Voice. With spirit.

Piano. *f*

mf

Key G. | s :— .s | d :d :d | m :m :m | r :— .r :r | f :— .f .f |
Go | pat - ter | to lub - bers and | swabs, do ye see, | A - bout
Why I | heard the | good chap - lain pa - | la - ver one day, | A - bout

| s :l :m | f :r :t, | d :— :l | :s, .s, | d :d :d | m :m :m |
dan - ger and fear and the | like, | A | | tight wat - ter boat and good
souls, hea - ven's mer - cy and such, | | And, my | tim - bers! what lin - go he'd

3

I said to our Poll — for d'ye see she would cry —
    When last we weighed anchor for sea,
What argufies snivelling and piping your eye?
    Why what a damn'd fool you must be!
Can't you see the world's wide and there's room for us all,
    Both for seamen and lubbers ashore?
And if to Old Davy I go, my friend Poll,
    You never will hear of me more.
What then? All's a hazard: Come don't be so soft:
    Perhaps I may laughing come back:
For, d'ye see, there's a cherub sits smiling aloft,
    To keep watch for the life of poor Jack.

4

D'ye mind me, a sailor should be every inch
    All as one as a piece of the ship,
And with her brave the world, not offering to flinch,
    From the moment the anchor's a — trip.
As for me, in all weathers, all times, sides and ends,
    Nought's a trouble from duty that springs,
For my heart is my Poll's, and my rhino's my friends.
    And as for my life, 'tis my king's.
E'en when my time comes, ne'er believe me so soft,
    As for grief to be taken aback,
For the same little cherub that sits up aloft
    Will look out a good berth for poor Jack!

THE MONKS OF OLD.

Words by WILLIAM JONES.
STEPHEN GLOVER.

3

And the abbot meek, with his form so sleek,
    Was the heartiest of them all:
And would take his place with a smiling face,
    When refection bell would call:
Then they sung and laugh'd and the rich wine quaff'd,
    Till they shook the olden wall!
And they laugh'd, ha! ha! and they quaff'd, ha! ha!
    Till they shook the olden wall.

4

Then say what you will, we'll drink to them still,
    For a jovial band they were;
And 'tis most true that a merrier crew
    Could not be found elsewhere;
For they sung and laugh'd and the rich wine quaff'd
    And lived on the daintiest cheer.
For they laugh'd, ha! ha! and they quaff'd, ha! ha!
    And lived on the daintiest cheer!

The Spider and the Fly.

(W. H. H.)

Chorus on next page.

3

"What very handsome wings you've got," said the spider to the fly,
"If I had such a pair, I'm sure, I in the air would fly!
'Tis useless all my wishing, and only idle talk:
You can fly up in the air so high while I'm obliged to walk."
    REFRAIN:— "Will you, will you."

4

"For the last time now I ask you, will you walk in, pretty fly?"
"No, if I do, may I be shot, I'm off, so now good bye."
Then up he springs, but both his wings were in the web caught fast—
The spider laugh'd. "Ha! ha! my boy. I've caught you safe at last."
    REFRAIN:— "Will you, will you."

5

Now all young men take warning by this foolish little fly:
Pleasure is the spider that to catch you fast will try:
And although you may be thinking that advice is quite a bore,
You're lost if you stand parleying outside of pleasure's door.
    REFRAIN:— "Will you, will you."

3
At length the wish'd for morrow,
   Broke thro' the hazy sky,
Absorb'd in silent sorrow,
   Each heav'd a bitter sigh.
The dismal wreck to view,
Struck horror in the crew,
As she lay, all that day,
In the Bay of Biscay, O!

4
Her yielding timbers sever,
   Her pitchy seams are rent,
When Heav'n all bounteous ever,
   Its boundless mercy sent.
A sail in sight appears,
We hail it with three cheers,
Now we sail, with the gale,
From the Bay of Biscay, O!

www.ingramcontent.com/pod-product-compliance
Lightning Source LLC
Chambersburg PA
CBHW022129160426
43197CB00009B/1213